People, Places and Policy

T0300091

Set within the context of UK devolution and constitutional change, *People, Places and Policy* offers important and interesting insights into 'place-making' and 'locality-making' in contemporary Wales. Combining policy research with policy-maker and stakeholder interviews at various spatial scales (local, regional, national), it examines the historical processes and working practices that have produced the complex political geography of Wales.

This book looks at the economic, social and political geographies of Wales, which in the context of devolution and public service governance are hotly debated. It offers a novel 'new localities' theoretical framework for capturing the dynamics of locality-making, to go beyond the obsession with boundaries and coterminous geographies expressed by policy-makers and politicians. Three localities – Heads of the Valleys (north of Cardiff), central and west coast regions (Ceredigion, Pembrokeshire and the former district of Montgomeryshire in Powys) and the A55 corridor (from Wrexham to Holyhead) – are discussed in detail to illustrate this and also reveal the geographical tensions of devolution in contemporary Wales.

This book is an original statement on the making of contemporary Wales from the Wales Institute of Social and Economic Research, Data and Methods (WISERD) researchers. It deploys a novel 'new localities' theoretical framework and innovative mapping techniques to represent spatial patterns in data. This allows the timely uncovering of both unbounded and fuzzy relational policy geographies, and the more bounded administrative concerns, which come together to produce and reproduce over time Wales' regional geography.

Martin Jones is Professor of Urban and Regional Political Economy, University of Sheffield, UK.

Scott Orford is Reader in GIS and Spatial Analysis, School of Planning and Geography, Cardiff University, Wales.

Victoria Macfarlane is Director of Operations at the Wales Institute of Social and Economic Research, Data and Methods (WISERD), Cardiff University, Wales.

Regions and Cities

Series Editor in Chief
Susan M. Christopherson, *Cornell University, USA*

Editors
Maryann Feldman, *University of Georgia, USA*
Gernot Grabher, *HafenCity University Hamburg, Germany*
Ron Martin, *University of Cambridge, UK*
Martin Perry, *Massey University, New Zealand*

In today's globalised, knowledge-driven and networked world, regions and cities have assumed heightened significance as the interconnected nodes of economic, social and cultural production, and as sites of new modes of economic and territorial governance and policy experimentation. This book series brings together incisive and critically engaged international and interdisciplinary research on this resurgence of regions and cities, and should be of interest to geographers, economists, sociologists, political scientists and cultural scholars, as well as to policy-makers involved in regional and urban development.

For more information on the Regional Studies Association visit www.regionalstudies.org

There is a **30% discount** available to RSA members on books in the Regions and Cities series, and other subject-related Taylor and Francis books and e-books including Routledge titles. To order just e-mail alex.robinson@tandf.co.uk, or phone on +44 (0) 20 7017 6924 and declare your RSA membership. You can also visit www.routledge.com and use the discount code: **RSA0901**

90. **Cities in Crisis**
    Socio-spatial impacts of the
    economic crisis in southern
    European cities
    *Edited by Jörg Knieling and
    Frank Othengrafen*

89. **Socio-Economic Segregation in
    European Capital Cities**
    East meets west
    *Edited by Tiit Tammaru, Szymon
    Marcinńczak, Maarten van Ham
    and Sako Musterd*

People, Places and Policy

Knowing contemporary Wales
through new localities

Edited by Martin Jones, Scott Orford and Victoria Macfarlane

Routledge
Taylor & Francis Group

LONDON AND NEW YORK

First published 2016 by Routledge

2 Park Square, Milton Park, Abingdon, Oxfordshire OX14 4RN
52 Vanderbilt Avenue, New York, NY 10017

Routledge is an imprint of the Taylor & Francis Group, an informa business

First issued in paperback 2019

British Library Cataloguing in Publication Data
A catalogue record for this book is available from the British Library

Library of Congress Cataloging in Publication Data
People, places and policy: knowing contemporary Wales through new
localities / edited by Martin Jones, Scott Orford and Victoria Macfarlane.
– First Edition.
Includes bibliographical references and index.
1. Wales–Economic conditions–21st century. 2. Wales–Politics and
government–21st century. I. Jones, Martin, 1970- editor. II. Orford, Scott,
editor. III. Macfarlane, Victoria, editor.
HC257.W3P46 2015
330.9429–dc23
2015008190

ISBN: 978-1-138-92520-5 (hbk)
ISBN: 978-0-367-87150-5 (pbk)

Typeset in Times New Roman
by Cenveo Publisher Services

Contents

Figures

Tables

Foreword

Overview of WISERD

The Wales Institute for Social and Economic Research, Data and Methods (WISERD) is a networked research institute spread across five higher education institutions in Wales: the universities of Aberystwyth, Bangor, Cardiff, South Wales and Swansea. WISERD was established in 2008 with funding from the Economic and Social Research Council (ESRC) and the Higher Education Funding Council for Wales (HEFCW). The Institute's research programme is being continued through a portfolio of major grants including a £7m investment from the ESRC in civil society research, funded through the Research Centres and Large Grants funding programme.

WISERD came together in response to the identification of a number of different priority areas for development within the social sciences in Wales and the UK more broadly. The Rhind Commission (2002) was set up to inquire into the state of social sciences in the UK (*Great Expectations: The Social Sciences in Britain*). It concluded that many of the most detailed and complex problems facing society in the twenty-first century call for investigation and analysis based upon the inter-disciplinary social sciences. The Commission's report suggested that universities needed to develop and support a *critical mass* of social sciences researchers, providing the basis for developing large, coherent, interdisciplinary teams, capable of bringing new approaches to these pressing social issues.

In Wales these issues were particularly prominent, with Rhind commenting specifically on the 'Welsh deficit' in UK-related funding (5 per cent of the population; 3 per cent of the funding); in addition, to this could be added the poor aggregate performance in ESRC competitions for research funds and PhD studentships. This view of Welsh social science was confirmed by the review undertaken by HEFCW into the *Current State of the Research Base in Wales*.

Taken together, these facts highlighted a critical weakness of the Welsh research infrastructure and its intellectual life, particularly in relation to the social sciences. This was seen as especially damaging given the wide range of economic, social and cultural issues in Wales that required, and continue to require, urgent social scientific investigation, and the growing need for an independent research base to inform the development of policy by the Welsh government. These issues were made more salient in the light of UK government's *Science and Innovation Investment Framework 2004–2014: Next Steps*.

This document recognised that some of the key challenges lie in promoting regional innovation in the context of strong regional discrepancies in research and development expenditure and the consequent significance of university-based regional activity.

WISERD came together out of a series of longstanding and distinctive research collaborations within Wales. The source of WISERD was an earlier bid for a Wales Institute of Economic and Social Research (WISER, submitted to the HEFCW Reconfiguration and Collaboration programme). The aim of WISER was to build capacity around usage of Welsh data and to carry out research into geography and locality, regeneration and Welsh governance. Following advice from HEFCW and the ESRC, and in response to the needs identified above, the proposal was revised to include colleagues with significant quantitative experience and to consider ways in which joint funding could be awarded through integration of the WISER bid with a continuation of the methodological and research capacity building work of the existing Cardiff-based unit, QUALITi, funded from 2005–08 by the ESRC as a Node of the National Centre for Research Methods (NCRM). By bringing QUALITi and WISERD together, WISERD was created. Since its inception, WISERD's key aims have been:

- To build and develop existing expertise in quantitative and qualitative research methods and methodologies;
- To develop and integrate a coherent set of research data relating to Wales;
- To build networks of researchers and research capacity across Wales in the economic and social sciences, as well as contributing to UK-wide research capacity building;
- To explore the relationships between research data, research methods and the development and understanding of policy;
- To develop a sustainable increase in the quantitative research base across the social sciences in Wales through academic appointments and training;
- To increase collaborative interdisciplinary research grant applications and interaction with policy-makers and the private sector through consultancy.

The research agenda of the first phase of WISERD was made up of five independent but interconnected research programmes: knowing localities and local knowledge in context; quantitative research; data integration and management; training and capacity building; and policy analysis and evaluation. This book presents findings from the WISERD Knowing Localities Research Programme, conceptualised and directed by Martin Jones, which has important implications for both regional studies and the devolved, and non-devolved, governance(s) of public policy in Wales.

Professor Huw Beynon
Cardiff University, WISERD Director, 2008–10

Contributors

Stephen Burgess, School of Planning and Geography, Cardiff University, Wales, UK.

Jesse Heley, Department of Geography and Earth Sciences, Aberystwyth University, Wales, UK.

Garry Higgs, Faculty of Computing, University of South Wales, Wales, UK.

Laura Jones, Department of Geography and Earth Sciences, Aberystwyth University, Wales, UK.

Robin Mann, School of Social Sciences, Bangor University, Wales, UK.

Kate Moles, School of Social Sciences, Cardiff University, Wales, UK.

Alexandra Plows, School of Social Sciences, Bangor University, Wales, UK.

Ian Stafford, Politics and International Relations, Cardiff University, Wales, UK.

Suzie Watkin, School of Art, Aberystwyth University, Wales, UK.

Michael Woods, Department of Geography and Earth Sciences, Aberystwyth University, Wales, UK.

Samuel Jones, Wales Institute of Social and Economic Research, Data and Methods (WISERD), Cardiff University, Wales, UK.

1 Introducing WISERD localities

Martin Jones, Victoria Macfarlane and Scott Orford

Introduction

> The governance of Wales has received more attention in the last twenty years than in the preceding centuries since the Acts of Union.
>
> (Williams, *Commission on Public Service Governance and Delivery*, Welsh Government, 2014: 114)

This book is situated within the context of devolution and constitutional change, which has certainly been a lively arena in recent years, especially in the context of the national referendum for Scottish independence, held on 18 September 2014, and the resulting 'devo-max' or 'devo-more' agenda (increased fiscal and financial autonomy resulting from the 'No' vote) and the corresponding future(s) of the United Kingdom after the 2015 General Election. The territories of Scotland, Wales, Northern Ireland and England – armed with a parliament (Scotland) and elected assemblies (Wales, Northern Ireland and London) – have certainly provided the basis for doing things differently and, in some cases, better. In Wales, devolution has certainly been the biggest shake-up to the British and UK state apparatus in recent times. In the words of Vernon Bogdanor, echoing the quote above, we are witnessing 'the most radical constitutional change this country has seen since the Great Reform Act of 1832' (1999: 1). The Great Reform Act set in motion our modern democratic state. The Labour Party (1997–2010) and the Conservative–Liberal Democrat Coalition Government (2010–2015) see devolution and constitutional change as an act of state modernisation to safeguard the socio-economic and political future of this United Kingdom. Our interest in this book, though, is with Wales and its reconstituted social, economic and political geographies, which, as noted by the quote above taken from the Williams Commission, are currently the subject of much heated debate. For the journalist Simon Jenkins (2014: 27), the 15 years of Welsh devolution, since the rise of Labour, have 'seen Wales transformed', with the Cardiff Assembly going through four elections and three first ministers, and with the interesting question raised of whether 'devolution has been good for Wales' or if Wales has merely played a role in the wider devolution domino-effect, which culminated in the Scottish referendum events of 2014 and the dominance of the Scottish National Party (SNP) in the 2015 General Election.

It is uncontested that Wales has a relatively short history of administrative devolution when compared to Scotland and Northern Ireland, if not England (see Osmond, 1978). Jenkins's cutting analysis makes some of this clear:

> After its conquest by Edward I in 1278, and its incorporation into England three centuries later by the Tudors, it had no governmental existence; it was 13 counties of 'England and Wales'. In 1965, as a sop to Welsh sentiment, Harold Wilson set up a Welsh Office with its own secretary of state; I remember hearing it described as the 'colonial office for Wales'. Then, in 1997, came Tony Blair's grand appeasement of Scottish nationalism, the offer of a devolved parliament which dragged Wales reluctantly in its train. The previous four-to-one rejection of devolution was converted onto a referendum majority of 50.3% for a new Welsh assembly, on a meagre 50% turnout. It was the most nervous possible mandate for self-government.
>
> (Jenkins 2014: 27)

Post-devolution Wales has accorded economic development a high political significance. Indeed, in the early days of devolution, Rhodri Morgan, when First Minister for Wales, famously argued that 'the most important task for any government is to create the conditions in which the economy can prosper' (*Western Mail*, 13 December 2001). Accordingly, the Welsh government's Treforest offices in south Wales, which deal with the Economy, Science and Transport (EST) portfolio, display bold bilingual white-on-blue signage above the green reception entrance, which reads:

> *Yn helpu I greu'r amodau iawn ar gyfer cynyddu swyddi, twf a chyfoeth*
> Helping to create the right conditions for increasing jobs, growth and wealth

Thus instead of being seen as effectively the regional office of Whitehall, where policy-making was essentially driven from London, devolution has offered the opportunity of bringing political scrutiny and public direction to the institutions of economic development. For much of the life of the first Assembly (1997–2001), the First Minister also held the Economic Development portfolio, illustrating its political importance and reinforcing those 'conditions' noted above (Goodwin et al., 2012).

The research contained in this chapter, which is situated in, and seeks to contribute to, this shifting state/space landscape, has been led by the Wales Institute for Social and Economic Research, Data and Methods (hereafter WISERD) Knowing Localities research team and contributed to by colleagues involved in each of the WISERD research programmes. During the mid- to late 1980s and early 1990s, 'locality' was *the* spatial metaphor to describe and explain the shifting world of the sub-national state and emerging, and subsequently rich, regional studies. This book argues that the resulting, often hot-headed, localities debate threw this (metaphorical) baby out with the (much baggage) bathwater and it urges a 'return to locality' to enlighten devolution and regional studies in Wales, to inform understandings of the above, and also beyond Wales in advanced capitalism. This chapter provides the platform for establishing these claims.

Spatial governance and Wales

The consolidation of Wales as a regional/national space of social and economic governance, with increasingly sharp territorial definition since the introduction of devolved government in 1999, has refocused attention on the dynamics of spatial difference within Wales. Persistent uneven geographies of socio-economic performance, as well as seemingly entrenched geographies of politi-cal and cultural difference, suggest the existence of 'locality effects' within Wales and present challenges for the delivery of policy. However, the shape of Wales's constituent localities is far from clear. Although Wales has a sub-regional tier of 22 local authorities, these have only been in existence since 1995, when they replaced a two-tier local government system established in 1974. Moreover, the administrative map is overlain and cross-cut by a plethora of other governmental bodies including health boards, police authorities, trans-port consortia and economic development partnerships – to name a few – that work to their own territorial remits. An attempt to produce a more nuanced and process-led representation of Wales's internal geography was made with the Wales Spatial Plan in 2004 (updated in 2008), but subsequent efforts to align the initially 'fuzzy' boundaries of the Spatial Plan regions with the hard boundaries of local authority areas demonstrates the accretional power of fixed institutional geographies in shaping the representation of localities (Haughton et al., 2009; see also Chapter 2).

These institutional geographies entered the central stage of political and economic analysis during 2013 and 2014. In April 2013 the Williams Commission on Public Service Governance and Delivery (chaired by Sir Paul Williams, a former Chief Executive of the NHS) was accordingly established by the First Minister for Wales and 'tasked with examining all aspects of govern-ance and delivery in the devolved public sector in Wales'. Rather than simplify the governance and understanding of public policy, devolution appears to have created much confusion and instilled over time what Jessop (2000) calls 'governance complexity'. In Wales, the effects of recession and austerity on public sector budgets have brought this to a head. By April 2013, the institu-tional landscape of Wales was evidenced by a littering of nearly 953 public bodies dealing with a range of economic and social concerns. These institutions have a complicated geography and occupy a number of spatial scales – national, regional, local, sub-local – and their interrelationships are far from clear. The Williams Commission sought to address this and their 347-page report is a fasci-nating account of this state of play after 15 years of relative autonomy from the shackles of Westminster and Whitehall. Following eight months of exhaustive analysis with policy-makers and the public through stakeholder engagement, they concluded that Wales seems to be in a position where (Welsh Government, 2014: 254):

- the design and structure of the public sector entails over-complex relationships between too many organisations, some of which are too small;
- it creates and sustains significant weaknesses in governance, performance management and organisational culture, or at least carries a significant risk of doing so;
- those weaknesses are mutually reinforcing and difficult to break from within;
- the consequence is poor and patchy performance because delivery mechanisms improve too slowly and inconsistently, and because there is no 'visible hand' driving improvement;
- strategic dialogue around reform of the system is sporadic and does not support the necessary shift towards co-production and prevention; and
- national policy initiatives may inadvertently compound the underlying problems they seek to solve.

In short, according to the Williams Commission, the public sector is too crowded and too complex to cope with the severe pressures that will continue to be placed on it. There are too many public organisations, and their interrelationships are too complex. This is true both of formal structures and their interrelationships, and less formal partnerships and collaborative arrangements; many public organisations in Wales are too small. While some of them may perform well (and some large organisations may perform badly), the smaller ones are suggested to face multiple and severe risks to governance and delivery which are likely to get worse in the medium term; many organisations are slow to respond to pressure for change.

The Williams Commission has offered 62 wide-ranging recommendations to address this. At a high level, aiming to 'break the cycle at every point' the report states:

Firstly, we propose that the complexity of the public sector is reduced by simplifying accountability, removing duplications, streamlining partnerships, making much better and more selective use of collaboration, and maximising the synergy between organisations, including service delivery and 'back-office' functions; *second we propose that the capacity of local authorities is increased by mergers between those that exist now.* That will combat the problems of small scale, and facilitate service integration and partnership working; third, we propose a range of measures to strengthen governance, scrutiny and accountability. Fourth, we propose new and more coherent approaches to leadership, to recruit the best, develop the leaders that we have and identify their successors. We also suggest that organisational cultures should be united around a shared, collaborative and citizen-centred set of public service values rather than narrow organisational objectives.

(Welsh Government, 2014: 259, emphasis added)

Recommendation two has understandably brought with it much excitement from players within the local state (see Welsh Local Government Association, 2014), as attention is focused on the 'spatially selective' realignment of local authorities, last reorganised two decades ago. The report recommends the new councils should be within current health board and police force areas and also not cross the geographical areas governing eligibility for EU aid. The report suggests, as a minimum, that the following local authorities should merge:

- Isle of Anglesey and Gwynedd
- Conwy and Denbighshire
- Flintshire and Wrexham
- Ceredigion and Pembrokeshire
- Neath Port Talbot and Bridgend
- Rhondda Cynon Taf and Merthyr Tydfil
- Cardiff and the Vale of Glamorgan
- Blaenau Gwent, Caerphilly and Torfaen
- Monmouthshire and Newport.

With Carmarthenshire, Powys and Swansea unchanged, this would yield 12 authorities. Using these mergers as 'building blocks' for the interlinking of changes to the systems, processes and cultures of the public sector, the report argues that there were other viable possibilities resulting in 11 or ten local authorities. Swansea could merge with Neath Port Talbot and Bridgend to form a single local authority, giving 11 local authorities in total. With Ceredigion effectively being recast as the 'new-Dyfed' (the administrative county of west Wales between 1974 and 1996), comments such as those below have been commonplace during 2014:

SUPERSTAR Elton John sang mournfully about the Circle of Life in the smash-hit musical The Lion King, but here in mid-Wales we have our own Circle of Strife roaring on. It is all down to yet another reorganisation of local government demanded by Wales's First Minister, Carwyn Jones. Years ago, big was beautiful and there was one giant county council, Dyfed, covering Ceredigion, Carmarthenshire and Pembrokeshire. But then in 1996, it was decided that small was beautiful, and the area was split back into three more manageable and hyper-local pieces. But now it appears that big is beautiful again and the number of councils in Wales faces being roughly halved from its current total of 22. If an all-encompassing Dyfed council is reborn, or a joint Ceredigion and Pembrokeshire council, there will be massive consequences for staff and services at Ceredigion County Council. And it has been warned that a Dyfed council would be particularly 'disastrous' for Aberystwyth, which could end up as just a far-flung outpost of a new south Wales-centred council. Now is the time for the circle to be squared once and for all so that people of Ceredigion do not suffer.

(Editorial, *Cambrian News*, 22 January 2014)

One could take issue with the principle and indeed costs of yet another round of local government restructuring (Welsh Local Government Association, 2014), which could be seen as displacing the problems of international/national recession and austerity into a specific problem of local state management (cf. Welsh Government, 2014: 108). The Williams Commission suggests that the cost of local authority mergers could be around £200 to £400 million, but will pay for itself within two to four years, through recurrent annual savings. We are more interested in notions and understandings of 'spatial complexity' that have been raised in the report and how they blatantly ignore complex nuanced processes of place-making and locality-making. According to the Williams Commission, the way in which the public sector has evolved also creates a risk that the boundaries of local and regional organisations are not coterminous, 'that is, they do not coincide' and 'a lack of coterminosity affects both service-providers and users [as] organisations which have to work across others' boundaries inevitably find it harder to form effective partnerships. In the same situation, citizens may find it confusing to understand which organisation is supposed to serve them, and harder to hold them to account' (ibid.: 32).

Although these statements hold some elements of truth, an obsession with boundaries, as opposed to an examination of the geographies of flows that produce and reproduce the various territorial shapes of contemporary Wales, hides the interrelated complexities that the Williams Commission sought to uncover. This is evident in a key statement on page 35: 'It is beyond our remit to consider detailed working practices within specific services; and there may well be sound operational reasons for these boundaries' (ibid.: 35). The WISERD Knowing Localities Research Programme was designed to address these contemporary, and other deep historical, concerns. The programme has aimed to develop understandings of the form and effects of localities in Wales and has developed analyses of localities that could serve to contextualise future case study research, after establishing a baseline of empirical research. It also aimed to explore locality effects on the processes and practices of policy-making and delivery and in wider social and economic experiences and dynamics through a series of focused pilot place-based studies. The remainder of this chapter outlines the notion of 'locality' and details the rationale behind the research and the methodology employed.

Overview of locality debate

As noted by Jones and Woods (2013), Massey's (1984) text *Spatial Divisions of Labour* was pivotal to starting what became the locality debate. This was written during an era of intense economic restructuring and challenged how geographers thought about 'the local' in an increasingly internationalising and globalising world fuelled by the collapse of Fordist-Keynesian compromises. The intellectual goal was to tease out the dialectic between space and place by looking at how *localities* were being positioned within, and in turn help to reposition, the changing national and international division of labour occurring at the time.

These scalar relationships were deemed to matter. For Massey (1991), 'the local in the global' is not simply an area one can draw a line around; instead, it is defined in terms of sets of social relations or processes under consideration. This highly influential 'new regional concept of localities' (Jonas, 1988) influenced two government-sponsored research initiatives in the UK, delivered through the Economic and Social Research Council – the Social Change and Economic Life programme and the Changing Urban and Regional Systems (CURS) programme. Both were given substantial funding and charged with remits to uncover the effects of international and global economic restructuring on local areas and why different responses and impacts were reported in different places.

In seeking to put 'the local' into 'the global', the CURS initiative set out to undertake theoretically informed empirical research in seven localities between 1985 and 1987. The goal was to examine the extent to which localities themselves could shape their own transformation and destiny as agents and not be passive containers for processes passed down from above.

As argued by Gregson (1987), Duncan and Savage (1991) and Barnes (1996), there is a fundamental difference between locality research (the CURS findings) and the resulting 'locality debate' across human geography and the social sciences, which was fuelled by a rethinking of how we theorised socio-spatial relations across these disciplines (itself bound up with a transition from Marxist to poststructuralist research enquiry) and shifting research methodologies and practices. The journal *Antipode*, followed by *Environment and Planning A*, between 1987 and 1991, published a series of often-heated exchanges on the whereabouts of localities (for summaries, compare Cooke, 2006; Jones and Woods, 2013).

Because CURS and the locality debate became so quickly conflated in these exchanges, the jettisoning of the notion of locality for some 25 years was somewhat inevitable. Locality was not held dear and its vagueness was captured by Duncan:

> Localities in the sense of autonomous subnational social units rarely exist, and in any case their existence needs to be demonstrated. But it is also misleading to use locality as a synonym for place or spatial variation. This is because the term locality inevitably smuggles in notions of social autonomy and spatial determinism, and this smuggling in excludes examination of these assumptions. It is surely better to use terms like town, village, local authority areas, local labour market or, for more general uses, place, area or spatial variation. These very usable terms do not rely so heavily on conceptual assumptions about space vis-à-vis society.
>
> (Duncan, 1989: 247)

The geographical problem at that time was that few cared to explain what locality, or the locality, or a locality, actually is. Locality was, for Duncan, 'an infuriating idea' (1989: 221); ill-defined, static and not sufficiently sensitive to the different forces making and fixing localities. Debates moved on and during the mid-1990s economic geographers became preoccupied not so much with localities *per se* but rather with the links between space and place as a way of looking at the 'local in the global'.

A 'new localities' research agenda

The WISERD Knowing Localities Research Programme was designed to pilot a 'new localities' research agenda within the context of post-devolution Wales. It argues that 'locality' remains an important vehicle in and through which to conduct social science research and, when re-energised through a multi-layered theoretical framework, 'locality' can enlighten and energise devolution studies, and certainly shine light on 'public services governance and delivery'. The locality concept was effectively a baby thrown out with the bathwater and a return to this spatial metaphor provides an important window on *knowing contemporary Wales* – the sub-title of this book.

Unlike earlier locality debates, our 'new localities' approach does not seek to adjudicate between these different representations of locality, but rather we recognise that all are valid ways of 'talking about locality', and each captures a different expression of locality. New localities are, therefore, multi-faceted and multi-dimensional. They are 'shape-shifters' whose form changes with the angle from which they are observed. As such, the identification of localities for research can be freed from the constraints of the rigid territoriality of administrative geography and should move beyond the reification of the local authority scale that was implicit in many previous locality studies.

The new localities approach accordingly focuses attention on processes of 'locality-making', or the ways in which semi-stabilised and popularly recognised representations of locality are brought into being through the moulding, manipulation and sedimentation of space within ongoing social, economic and political struggles (Jonas, 2012). Indeed, it is in these 'acts of locality-making' that localities are transformed from mere points of location (a description of where research was conducted) to socio-economic–political assemblages that provide an analytical framework for research.

The attributes of localities then do not easily translate into discrete territorial units with fixed boundaries. Labour market areas overlap, as do shopping catchment areas; residents may consider themselves to be part of different localities for different purposes and at different times; the reach of a town as an education centre may be different to its reach as an employment centre; and so on. The boundaries that might be ascribed to a locality will vary depending on the issue(s) in question (Warde, 1989).

All this has a bearing on how localities are identified, defined and constructed for case study research. This logically leads us to start by identifying localities by their cores – whether these be towns or cities or geographical areas – rather than as bounded territories, and working outwards to establish an understanding of their coherences. This process necessarily requires the use of a mixed methods approach, combining cartographic and quantitative data on material geographies; with qualitative evidence of locality-making in performed patterns and relations. However, this is not intended to act as an exercise in boundary-drawing. While it is possible to identify fixed territorial limits for the reach of a locality with respect to certain governmental competences or policy fields, it should also be understood that all proxy boundaries will be permeable to a degree, and that localities may be configured differently depending on the object of enquiry.

WISERD Localities Research Programme

Research was undertaken in a series of localities between 2009 and 2011, chosen to reflect the diversity of territories, places, scales and networks in contemporary Wales. The three localities were also selected to give contrasting insights into the geographies and area vision of the Wales Spatial Plan.

The chosen localities were: the Heads of the Valleys region north of Cardiff; the central and west coast region (comprising the unitary authorities of Ceredigion and Pembrokeshire and the former district of Montgomeryshire in Powys); and the A55 corridor from Wrexham to Holyhead in north Wales – see Figure 1.1. The rationales for selecting and defining these three localities are discussed in detail in chapters 4, 5 and 6, where the localities themselves are analysed. It was also appreciated early on that in order to operationalise the research, it would be necessary to use some definition of bounded territory in the initial constructions of the localities for various practical and pragmatic reasons relating to the availability of published data, the function and discharge of policy-related practices and governance that are threaded through the concept of new localities and as a useful and systematic approach of structuring the methodology. It was also appreciated that these definitions based on bounded territories were not fixed and that the concepts of locality in terms of unbounded and fuzzy spaces would be explored throughout the research and through analysis of the data. The subsequent chapters explore these issues through various data, socio-economic issues and policy perspectives and will be drawn together in the conclusion.

In accordance with a mixed methods approach, the research programme was split into three stages:

1. Completion of a series of quantitative baseline data audits.
2. Completion of a series of qualitative stakeholder interviews.
3. Analysis of the research findings.

For consistency's sake, and to minimise contradictions between data sources and the stakeholder interviews, all the data and analysis relates to either the duration of the study (2009 to 2010) or prior to the commencement of the study. Data collected after the end of the study period that has since become available has not been included in the analysis or discussions.

As a starting point, a series of baseline audits were undertaken using existing published statistics related to each of the three localities. The audits were structured according to a series of eight thematic policy areas. These were identified by the Welsh government and WISERD as reflecting the range of key devolved and non-devolved policy areas. These also map onto existing networks and centres

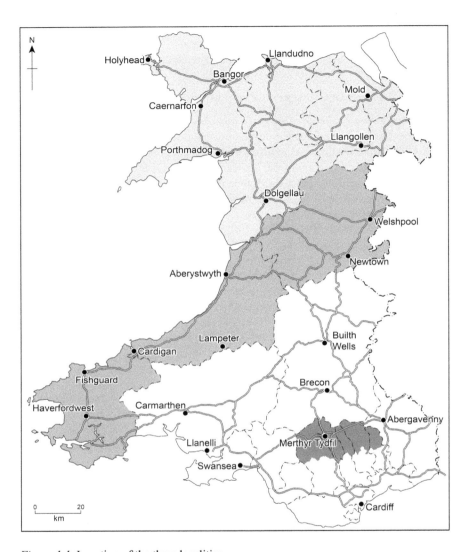

Figure 1.1 Location of the three localities

Source: Mastermap Layer@Crown Copyright/database right 2010.
An Ordnance Survey/EDINA supplied service.

of excellence of academic research in Wales and were deemed to be of specific relevance to the selected localities. The themes are as follows:

- Education and young people
- Crime, public space and policing
- Health, well-being and social care

- Language, citizenship and identity
- Employment and training
- Environment, tourism and leisure
- Economic development and regeneration
- Housing and transport.

The audits ensured that the research team had an in-depth knowledge of how specific services were operating in each of the localities. They were also used to provide a reference point in understanding how the policy themes interacted with the localities and vice versa – an approach, as noted above, that was out of the remit of the Williams Commission. To help put the localities into a wider context, and provide a bridge between them, an all-Wales audit was also undertaken in parallel that investigated published data relating to the eight policy areas at a variety of spatial scales. In addition to the baseline audits, a series of eight policy briefing documents were also developed, providing information on each of the substantive policy themes listed above.

A total of 120 stakeholder interviews were carried out in the three selected WISERD localities. The aim of the interviews was to explore the 'experiential materialities' of the three localities in regards to specific policy themes: how within each of these areas key local public agencies, organisations, groups and individuals define the space(s) in which they operate, concretise it (them) through their day-today practice, define the main problems to be tackled and in the process help construct the idea of 'locality'. In short, we were interested in the lived spatial policy-worlds occupied by policy-makers and those on the receiving end of their endeavours.

The interviews were designed to add depth and richness to the quantitative baseline locality-specific data, and to afford a more detailed and multi-dimensional picture of all three localities in the wider context of Wales as a whole. In addition to providing qualitative data that would support, question or otherwise dialogue with numeric data, it was felt that lengthy, semi-structured interviews with key stakeholders working within the localities would, in their own right, afford a valuable data resource, enabling analysis of 'place-shaping' through ground-level professional practices at a number of scales and levels.

The stakeholders selected for interview correspond to the eight thematic policy areas, which had also informed the prior cross-Wales baseline data-mapping audits. To identify the stakeholders, two unitary authorities in the Central and west Coast (Ceredigion, Pembrokeshire) and the A55 corridor (Gwynedd, Wrexham) localities and three unitary authorities (Blaenau Gwent, Merthyr Tydfil, Rhondda Cynon Taf) in the Heads of the Valleys locality were selected and the stakeholders mapped across the seven unitary authorities by their role in the organisations. Two tiers of stakeholder were identified: Tier 1, who were unitary authority directors and service managers, and Tier 2, who were managers in other bodies in partnership with unitary authorities with responsibility for service delivery and policy. Table 1.1 provides a summary of the number of interviewees in each unitary authority by tier. The majority of the stakeholders

Table 1.1 A summary of the stakeholder interviews by unitary authority and tier

Locality	Unitary authority	Tier	Number of interviewees
Central and west	Ceredigion	1	8
Coast	Ceredigion	2	5
	Pembrokeshire	1	7
	Pembrokeshire	2	3
	Other	1	1
	Other	2	12
A55 corridor	Gwynedd	1	6
	Gwynedd	2	16
	Wrexham	1	8
	Wrexham	2	5
The Heads of the	Blaenau Gwent	1	6
Valleys	Blaenau Gwent	2	5
	Merthyr Tydfil	1	5
	Merthyr Tydfil	2	5
	Rhondda Cynon Taf	1	9
	Rhondda Cynon Taf	2	11
	Other	2	8

were based within a unitary authority, but some worked for organisations that cut across authorities, such as the Health Service or Environment Agency, and these are identified as 'other'. In total, 36 (30 per cent) stakeholders were interviewed in the Central and West Coast Locality (CWCL), 16 at Tier 1 and 20 at Tier 2; 35 (30 per cent) stakeholders were interviewed in the A55 corridor locality, 14 at Tier 1 and 21 at Tier 2; and 49 (40 per cent) stakeholders were interviewed in the Heads of the Valleys locality, 20 at Tier 1, 29 at Tier 2.

The interviews were undertaken, where possible, in the stakeholder's place of work by researchers who had experience of interviewing. The focus of the interviews was on the role of the stakeholder within their policy area and how their understanding of their 'patch' or the locality in which they worked influenced what they did. Hence, the interviews had a strong geographical slant, with the interviewees encouraged to discuss the places important in their work. All the interviewees signed a consent form agreeing that the interview material could be analysed and attributions made in publications on the condition that the participants remained anonymous. The interviews were recorded and sent for transcription by a professional company which returned the interviews as word documents in a standard format. These were then coded and analysed by qualitative researchers using a Computer Assisted Qualitative Data Analysis Software (CAQDAS) package, in this case Atlas.ti.

Using a qualitative geographic information system (GIS) approach, places mentioned in the interviews were geo-referenced and mapped as points and one standard deviation spatial ellipses were created to allow the patterns defined by the places to be described statistically and visually. A one standard deviational ellipse represents approximately 68 per cent of the points and is centred on the mean of the point pattern, with its long axis in the direction of the maximum dispersion and its short axis in the direction of the minimum dispersion. Hence, an ellipse is produced if the points have a directional component, otherwise the ellipse will be more or less circular. One advantage of the spatial ellipse is that they are good for comparing point patterns without revealing the locations of any points and thus there is minimal risk of disclosure. More detail on the methodology of the WISERD Localities Research Programme can be found in Dicks (2012).

Conclusions

The new localities methodology as defined and summarised above, we argue, provides the opportunity to carry out policy-focused research in and on Wales, which is ideally suited to the complexities and contingencies of the post-devolution landscape. The following chapters will describe in greater depth the policy landscape of Wales; will outline Wales from a statistical point of view; and will look in greater depth at the three locality study areas; before outlining some possibilities for future research.

Chapter 2 provides an overview of four overarching themes that have shaped the wider policy landscape within Wales since the introduction of devolution proper in 1999. These are: the changing nature of the institutional character of devolved governance within Wales; the reshaping of the political and electoral identity of Wales since devolution; the evolving shape of intergovernmental relations between the local and the newly devolved centre; and the strategic policy context that has framed attempts to develop a spatially sensitive approach to policy integration across Wales.

Chapter 3 acts as precursor to, and a bridge between, the more in-depth exploration of Wales (chapters 4, 5, 6) and provides a national context to the smaller-scale studies that follow in the book. The chapter details the very diverse and distinctive geographical differences in population and other socio-economic and cultural characteristics in Wales. It does this through the use of official statistics (prior to the 2011 Census), presented at a variety of spatial scales, and supports this with conventional maps, cartograms, graphs and tables. The chapter highlights a strong thematic socio-spatial patterning within Wales, which is investigated in detail in the locality research.

Chapter 4, the first of the locality case study chapters, provides a detailed critical analysis of how the Heads of the Valleys has been constructed as a policy area and territory by the Welsh government and previous policy-makers. It demonstrates the contradictions and tensions that have shaped the locality during almost 100 years of deindustrialisation and how the locality has provided opportunities for state-fostered economic and social development.

Chapter 5 is about north Wales, specifically an A55 corridor analysis of socio-economic change and development in the twenty-first century. This chapter serves as a way of displaying both the connected and peripheral geographies of this locality; north east Wales is a space for multiple cross-border interactions, as is the maritime flows from Holyhead, whereas parts of north west Wales have a deeper stasis. The impacts that this has on culture, language and identity are discussed in the chapter.

Chapter 6, on mid Wales, is the last of the three locality chapters. It offers a reading of a CWCL – a predominately rural area arcing across central Wales and the south west seaboard, extending from St David's Head to the Shropshire border and from the Preseli Mountains and Teifi Valley to the Berwyn range and river Dyfi. The challenges of rurality are discussed in the chapter, not just in terms of economic challenges and opportunities, but also how this is managed spatially.

The conclusion to the book, Chapter 7, comments on the suitability of our collected data and official sources for capturing our ability to know Wales through the intersections between people, policy and place. It then returns to the 'new locality' conceptual framework and considers its usefulness for undertaking locality research in Wales, particularly providing insights into the contemporary devolution challenges of city-region building, which is being introduced to agglomerate economic activity in the face of globalisation and the shake-out of austerity.

References

Barnes, T. (1996) *Logics of Dislocation: Models, Metaphor and Meanings of Economic Space*. New York: Guilford.

Bogdanor, V. (1999) *Devolution in the United Kingdom*. Oxford: Oxford University Press.

Cooke, P. (2006) Locality debates. *Mimeograph*. Centre for Advanced Urban Studies. Cardiff: Cardiff University.

Dicks, B. (2012) 'Construction of the stakeholder matrix, planning and conduct of the interviews and analysis of the transcripts', *WISERD Methods Briefing Series*.

Duncan, S. (1989) 'What is locality?', in Peet, R. and Thrift, N. (eds), *New Models in Geography: Volume Two*. London: Unwin Hyman.

Duncan, S. and Savage, M. (1991) 'New perspectives on the locality debate', *Environment and Planning A*, 23, 155–64.

Goodwin, M., Jones, M. and Jones, R. (2012) *Rescaling the State: Devolution and the Geographies of Economic Governance*. Manchester: Manchester University Press.

Gregson, N. (1987) 'The CURS initiative: some further comments', *Antipode*, 19, 364–70.

Haughton, G., Allmendinger, P., Counsell, D. and Vigar, G. (2009), *The New Spatial Planning: Territorial Management with Soft Spaces and Fuzzy Boundaries*. London: Routledge.

Jenkins, S. (2014) 'A chance for Wales: can the slumbering dragon awake?', *Guardian*, 30 September, 27–9.

Jessop, B. (2000) 'Governance failure', in Stoker, G. (ed.), *The New Politics of British Local Governance*. Basingstoke: Macmillan.

Jonas, A. (1988) 'A new regional geography of localities', *Area*, 20, 101–10.

Jonas, A. (2012) 'Region and place: regionalism in question', *Progress in Human Geography*, 36, 263–72.

Jones, M. and Woods, M. (2013) 'New localities', *Regional Studies*, 47, 29–42.

Massey, D. (1984) *Spatial Divisions of Labour: Social Structures and the Geography of Production*. Basingstoke: Macmillan.

Massey, D. (1991) 'The political place of locality studies', *Environment and Planning A*, 267–81.

Osmond, J. (1978) *Creative Conflict: The Politics of Welsh Devolution*. London: Routledge.

Warde, A. (1989) 'A recipe for pudding: a comment on locality', *Antipode*, 21, 274–81.

Welsh Government (2014) *Commission on Public Service Governance and Delivery: Full Report*. Cardiff: Welsh Government.

Welsh Local Government Association (2014) *Report of the Commission on Public Service Governance and Delivery*. Press Release, 20 January. Cardiff: WLGA.

2 Reframing the devolved policy landscape in Wales

Ian Stafford

Introduction

The constitutional reform programme pursued by the Labour Government following the 1997 General Election fundamentally recast territorial politics and administration within the United Kingdom (UK). The introduction of devolved administrations in Scotland, Wales and Northern Ireland, the regional agenda pursued in England and the creation of an elected mayor in London challenged the already somewhat over-stated and loosely defined characterisation of the UK as a paragon of the unitary state model. Indeed, Bradbury and Le Galés (2008: 203) reflected that 'gone are the days when the view could still go relatively unchallenged that the UK was a unitary and centralised state, mostly homogeneous and integrated despite minor territorial differences'. The legislative approach to devolution adopted by the Labour Government built a significant degree of asymmetry into the devolved settlement reflecting the contrasting pre-devolution political and institutional contexts in England, Northern Ireland, Scotland and Wales. Furthermore, inherent in this model of devolution was the scope for the continuous development of the legislative competencies and functions of devolved administrations. The design of the original devolved settlement within Wales provided perhaps the clearest example of this incremental approach to the further development of devolution. Indeed, it was the former Secretary of State for Wales, Ron Davies, who famously stated that devolution was 'a process' and 'not an event' or 'a journey with a fixed end-point' (Davies, 1999: 15). The first decade and more of devolution in Wales has provided ample evidence to underpin Davies' original claim.

The introduction of the National Assembly for Wales in 1999 fundamentally reshaped the institutional and political landscape of Wales but it was by no means the only element of this process. For example, the reorganisation of local government in 1996 and the considerable institutional churn of arms-length and non-governmental agencies or quangos, such as the Welsh Development Agency (WDA) and Education and Learning Wales (ELWa) also played a key role in moulding the policy context in contemporary Wales (Pemberton, 2000; Morgan, 1997; Jones et al., 2005). However, Bradbury and Stafford (2008: 67) note that the introduction of devolution raised key questions regarding the relative autonomy to develop public policy in Wales – the extent of policy competencies, the institutional and policy community capacity to make policy related to Welsh needs and the political ends to which policy would be put. Further questions can be added across a myriad of research areas including the changing shape of public attitudes to devolution, the shifting political and electoral character of Wales and the evolving relationship between the newly created devolved tier and existing levels of government. It is clearly beyond the scope of this introductory chapter to chart the entire story of devolution in Wales – the ebb and flow of party politics, the developments in specific policy fields and the significant debates around the nature of the devolved settlement. Instead, this chapter provides a brief introduction to four overarching themes which have shaped the wider policy landscape within Wales since the introduction of devolution in 1999 and which echo many of the issues highlighted in chapters elsewhere in this volume: the changing nature of the institutional character of devolved governance within Wales; the reshaping of the political and electoral identity of Wales since devolution; the evolving shape of intergovernmental relations between the local and newly devolved 'centre'; and the strategic policy context which has framed attempts to develop a spatially sensitive approach to policy integration across Wales.

Devolution as 'a process, not an event': the evolution of the Welsh government and the National Assembly for Wales

As noted in the previous chapter, prior to the introduction of devolution in 1999, the primary focus of territorial governance within Wales centred on the Secretary of State for Wales and the Welsh Office, established by the Labour Government in 1964 to 'express the voice of Wales' (Bogdanor, 1999: 160). The responsibilities of the Welsh Office were initially limited to executive powers in a narrow range of policy fields but both Labour and Conservative governments adopted an approach to the territorial management of Wales which saw these functions steadily increase over the period (Deacon, 2002; Bradbury, 1997, 1998). Although the Welsh Office had grown in terms of its financial importance and administrative responsibilities, concerns remained regarding the democratic accountability of the department and, by the mid-1990s, these tensions were exacerbated by the increase of arms-length, non-governmental agencies or quangos within Wales (Jones, 2000). These concerns were further enhanced by the decline in the Conservative Party's share of the vote in Wales and the growth of the perception that the interests of Wales were not being recognised by a Westminster government whose mandate was primarily based on English votes (Morgan and Roberts, 1993; Chaney et al., 2001). The perceived democratic deficit within Wales played a key role in underpinning the inclusion of Welsh devolution as part of the Labour Party's proposed constitutional reform programme ahead of the 1997 General Election (Bradbury, 1998). However, the introduction of devolution was predicated on gaining a simple majority in a pre-legislative referendum and it was by no means certain that this was guaranteed. The Welsh electorate had overwhelmingly rejected the previous attempt to introduce political devolution in 1979 (20.3 per cent voting 'yes', 79.7 per cent voting 'no'). In the event the proposals outlined within the White Paper *A Voice for Wales* received a wafer thin majority in the 1997 referendum (50.3 per cent voting 'yes', 49.7 per cent voting 'no') (Wyn Jones and Lewis, 2002).

The original model of 'executive devolution' introduced by the Government of Wales Act 1998 did not provide the National Assembly for Wales with any primary legislative or tax-raising powers but transferred the limited secondary and executive functions previously exercised by the Secretary of State for Wales and the Welsh Office. This 'patchwork of powers' was widely criticised for introducing a legally, administratively and constitutionally complex and fragmented devolution settlement (Williams, 2002; Navarro and Lambert, 2005; Rawlings 2003). Furthermore, attempts to draw down further powers from the UK level on a piecemeal basis through Wales-only bills or Wales-only clauses in UK or England and Wales bills were highly dependent on the goodwill of Whitehall departments and the vagaries of the legislative timetable at Westminster (Bradbury and Stafford, 2010). In addition, the design of the Assembly as a body corporate, combining the legislative and executive functions rather than separating them, was the focus of much debate in the early years of the Assembly. The former Secretary of State for Wales and architect of the original devolved settlement, Ron Davies, had emphasised the importance of the body corporate design in delivering a form of 'new politics' characterised by an inherent 'inclusiveness' which was missing from the adversarial Westminster model (Chaney and Fevre, 2001). However, the early experiences of the Assembly highlighted the fundamental tensions between the cabinet and committee models of administration which had shaped the hybrid design of the Government of Wales Act 1998 (Rawlings, 1998). Notably, the Assembly's Subject Committees, envisaged by the Assembly's First Secretary, Alun Michael, as the 'engine room' of the Assembly, combined three overlapping and at times potentially conflicting roles: the scrutiny of the administration, policy-making and dealing with subordinate or secondary legislation (Rawlings, 2003).[1]

The Labour Party's failure to secure a majority in the 1999 Assembly elections provided an important catalyst for these reform debates in the first term of the Assembly and these provided a central element of the partnership agreement between Welsh Labour and the Welsh Liberal Democrats in October 2000 (Bradbury, 2008). Initially, the reform agenda was taken forward by the cross-party Assembly Review of Procedure, announced by Michael's successor, Rhodri Morgan, in July 2000. The Review's recommendations, adopted unanimously by the Assembly, led to the de facto separation of the executive and legislature via the creation of the Welsh Assembly Government (National Assembly for Wales, 2002). The Labour–Liberal Democrat partnership agreement also led to the creation of the Richard Commission to review the adequacy of the depth and breadth of the Assembly's powers and its electoral arrangements (Commission on the Powers and Electoral Arrangements, 2004). The Commission recommended in its final report, published in March 2004, that the Assembly should move to full legislative powers by 2011 and that, in the meantime, its existing powers should be expanded as far as possible. The report also identified the desirability of tax-varying powers and that an increase in the Assembly's membership to 80 would be required to reflect its enhanced legislative powers (Commission on the Powers and Electoral Arrangements, 2004: 262).

The UK Government's response to the calls for reform were outlined in the June 2005 White Paper, *Better Governance for Wales* and introduced via the Government of Wales Act 2006 (Wales Office, 2005). The UK Government adopted a phased expansion of the Assembly's law-making powers but largely ignored the Richard Commission's recommendations around tax-varying powers and the size of the Assembly (Johnson, 2008). The first proposed phase committed Whitehall departments, within the context of the existing settlement, to enhance the use of framework legislation by delegating 'maximum discretion' to the National Assembly in drafting primary legislation. The second 'interim' phase, outlined in Part 3 of the 2006 Act, introduced procedures enabling Parliament to give the Assembly 'powers to modify legislation or make new provision on specific Matters or within defined areas of policy within the Fields in which the Assembly currently exercises functions'. These arrangements provided the Assembly with bounded competence to pass legislation via Assembly Measures in relation to specific matters contained within 20 broadly defined fields outlined within Schedule 5 of the 2006 Act (see Table 2.1). The third and final stage, outlined within Part 4 of the 2006 Act, centred on the devolution of 'general powers to make primary legislation in those areas where functions have already been devolved' following approval from the Welsh

Table 2.1 Twenty policy fields listed in Schedule 5 of the Government of Wales Act 2006

Field 1: Agriculture, fisheries, forestry and rural development
Field 2: Ancient monuments and historic buildings
Field 3: Culture
Field 4: Economic development
Field 5: Education and training
Field 6: Environment
Field 7: Fire and rescue services and promotion of fire safety
Field 8: Food
Field 9: Health and health services
Field 10: Highways and transport
Field 11: Housing
Field 12: Local government
Field 13: National Assembly for Wales
Field 14: Public administration
Field 15: Social welfare
Field 16: Sport and recreation
Field 17: Tourism
Field 18: Town and country planning
Field 19: Water and flood defence
Field 20: Welsh language

Source: HM Government (2006).

electorate in a referendum (Wales Office, 2005: 9). However, the White Paper and 2006 Act did not prescribe a fixed timetable for the transition to the final stage and therefore introduced what was effectively an open-ended process.

The Part 3 arrangements were introduced at the beginning of the third Assembly term and provided the Assembly with two primary routes to expand its legislative competence: i) 'framework powers' or 'measure-making clauses' contained within UK legislation and ii) Legislative Competence Orders (LCOs) initiated by the Assembly and approved by the UK Parliament. These measures were designed to respond to the 2005 White Paper's objective to 're-balance legislative authority towards the Assembly, without affecting the overall constitutional supremacy of Parliament' (Wales Office, 2005: 2). The 2006 Act was heralded by the then Secretary of State for Wales, Peter Hain, as providing 'a new constitutional settlement that will endure for a generation or more' (Wales Office, 2007: 3). However, these arrangements, particularly the LCO process, were subject to a great deal of criticism and were increasingly perceived as an unsustainable compromise (Wigley, 2006; Hill et al., 2008; Navarro and Lambert, 2009; Miers, 2011). Once again the Labour Party's failure to secure a majority at the 2007 Assembly elections short-circuited the process and the resulting *One Wales* agreement between Plaid Cymru and Labour included the commitment 'to proceed to a successful outcome of a referendum for full law-making powers under Part 4 as soon as practicable, at or before the end of the Assembly term (2007–11)' (Wales Labour Party and Plaid Cymru, 2007: 6). The commitment to hold a referendum on further law-making powers led to the establishment of the All Wales Convention to assess the effectiveness of the Part 3 arrangements and the levels of public support for full law-making powers.

The All Wales Convention's report, published in November 2009, argued that the proposed Part 4 arrangements offered 'substantial advantage' over the status quo and that, although the electorate appeared to have 'limited knowledge' of the procedures and issues, a 'yes' vote in a referendum was obtainable (All Wales Convention, 2009: 6–7). The 2010 campaign was characterised by a high degree of consensus among the political elite within Wales (for an overview of the referendum campaigns and result, see Stafford, 2011, and Wyn Jones and Scully, 2012). The result of the 2011 referendum marked a significant shift in public support for devolution (63.5 per cent voting 'yes', 36.5 per cent voting 'no') and to a degree laid to rest the ghosts of the failed 1979 referendum and narrow 'yes' vote at the 1997 referendum (National Assembly for Wales, 2011a). However, a key feature of the referendum result was the relatively low turnout, 35.6 per cent of registered voters, in comparison to past referendums within the UK. The transition to Part 4 arrangements significantly expanded the Assembly's legislative competence and provided the Assembly with general legislative authority to introduce 'Assembly Acts' within these areas without reference to Parliament. The extent to which the further strengthening of the National Assembly provides a degree of stability within the devolved settlement remains open to question; for example, in October 2011 the UK Coalition announced the creation of the Silk Commission, chaired by Paul Silk, former Clerk to the National Assembly for Wales, to review the case for devolving fiscal powers and the powers of the National Assembly in general. Therefore, the characterisation of Welsh devolution as 'a process not an event' appears to be as relevant in the fourth term of the National Assembly as it was in 1999 – certainly, the recommendations by the Silk Commission in its two reports published in November 2012 and March 2014 and the UK Government's command paper 'Powers with a Purpose', published in 2015 following the Coalition Government's St David's Day commitment to respond to the narrow no vote in the September 2014 Scottish referendum (see Commission on Devolution in Wales, 2012, 2014; HM Government 2015) could ultimately bring new opportunities for awakening the 'slumbering dragon', as Jenkins (2014: 27) puts it.

Quiet earthquakes and the end of Labour hegemony: the changing political and electoral landscape of Wales

The question of the potential distinctiveness of Welsh politics, the character of Welsh national identity and its relationship to the Welsh language in different parts of Wales, and the relationship between notions of 'Welshness' and 'Britishness' have been recurring themes in academic debates (Balsom, 1985; Balsom et al., 1983, 1984; Aitchison and Carter, 2004; Coupland et al., 2005; Day and Thompson, 1999; Housley et al., 2009; Evans, 2007; Wyn Jones, 2001; Davies, 2005; Bradbury and Andrews, 2010). Wyn Jones (2001: 38) noted that the national identity of Wales's population was 'far from homogeneous' and that, although a majority identify themselves as being both Welsh and British, this differs 'in degrees that vary not only from person to person, but also from context to context'. Furthermore, national identity is further complicated by substantial minorities who feel exclusively Welsh or British, the one fifth of the population who speak Welsh – which has been traditionally associated with an intensification of national sentiment – and the further substantial minority of the population born outside of Wales, mostly in England. Perhaps the most influential study of perceptions of national identity within Wales and its relationship with political identity and language has been Balsom's (1985) characterisation of the 'Three-Wales model'. He identifies three 'distinct and identifiable sociolinguistic groups': i) a Welsh-speaking, Welsh-identifying group centred upon the north and west of Wales – designated as *Y Fro Gymraeg*; ii) a Welsh-identifying, non-Welsh-speaking group most prevalent in the 'traditional' south Wales area of the valleys and west towards Swansea – designated as *Welsh Wales*; and iii) a British-identifying, non-Welsh-speaking group which dominates the remainder of east Wales, coastal south east Wales and west Wales around Pembrokeshire – designated as *British Wales* (Balsom, 1985: 6). In terms of political behaviour, these groups are reflected in the core areas of support for the main political parties; for example, Plaid Cymru's support is centred on the Welsh-speaking, Welsh-identifying group and the Conservatives and to a lesser extent the Liberal Democrats on the British-identifying, non-Welsh-speaking group. Although the 'Three-Wales model' has been subject to a range of critiques in recent years, it remains highly influential in terms of understanding national identity and political behaviour in Wales (see Coupland et al., 2005, for a useful critique).

A key theme highlighted by Balsom's analysis was that only the Labour Party was successfully able to draw support across the three ethnolinguistic groups identified within the 'Three-Wales' model (for an updated analysis, see Wyn Jones, 2001). The support for the Labour Party across identity groups can be seen as reflecting the party's traditional hegemonic position within Wales. Wyn Jones and Scully (2008) note that for much of the twentieth century party politics within Wales has been characterised by a strong one-partyism, initially via the Liberals and since the 1920s through the Labour Party. Indeed, they argue that in many areas, notably the south Wales valleys, the party remained virtually unchallenged. Trystan et al. (2003: 638) argue that there was little to suggest that devolution would lead to a major change in the electoral landscape in Wales despite the negative headlines created by the acrimonious leadership battle between Alun Michael and Rhodri Morgan following Ron Davies' resignation and the mixed electoral system made up of 40 constituency seats and 20 proportional regional list seats. However, the result of the 1999 Assembly election, characterised as a 'quiet earthquake' by Plaid Cymru's Dafydd Wigley, seriously challenged Labour's hegemony (see Table 2.2). Labour's proportion of the vote dropped from almost 55 per cent in the 1997 General Election to 37.6 per cent in the constituency vote and 35.4 per cent in the regional list vote (Wyn Jones and Scully, 2006). The main beneficiary of Labour's poor performance were Plaid Cymru, who achieved their best election performance and won previous Labour strongholds in the south Wales valleys, such as the Rhondda and Islwyn. However, a notable feature of the first and subsequent Assembly elections has been the relative apathy of the Welsh electorate towards devolution, highlighted by the low levels of turnout (46 per cent in 1999; 38 per cent in 2003; 43 per cent in 2007; and 41 per cent in 2011).

The surprising nature of the 1999 election result led to a variety of explanations being offered by commentators. Although it is hard to disagree with the argument

Table 2.2 National Assembly for Wales election results, 1999

	Cons	Lab	Lib Dem	Plaid	Other	Total
Seats						
Constituency seats	1	27	3	9	0	40
Regional seats	8	1	3	8	0	20
Total seats won	9	28	6	17	0	60
Constituency ballot						
Votes (000s)	162	385	138	291	48	1023
Share of vote %	15.8	37.6	13.5	28.4	4.8	100
Regional ballot						
Votes (000s)	168	362	128	312	50	1020
Share of vote %	16.5	35.5	12.5	30.6	5.0	100

Source: House of Commons (1999).

that the Labour Party's performance was undermined by a range of internal factors, the assertion that the devolved elections represented 'second order elections' characterised by low turnout and a high level of protest votes is more problematic (Balsom, 2000). Trystan et al. (2003: 648) argue that 'the slump in Labour support and the dramatic advance for Plaid Cymru that was experienced reflected not so much a generalised alienation from the Labour Party among the Welsh electorate as a more specific disinclination to support the party in this particular electoral context'. Thus, the introduction of devolution can be seen to have fundamentally reframed the political and electoral context within Wales, highlighted by Assembly election results since 1999. The Assembly elections in 2003, 2007 and 2011 appear to demonstrate the decline of Labour's hegemony and 'one-partyism' within Wales (Table 2.3). Wyn Jones and Scully (2003) note, for example, that although Labour triumphantly reclaimed its historical strongholds and gained a working majority, its increase in share of the vote was actually fairly modest. However, a clear result of the realignment of Welsh politics following devolution has been the significant changes in the language and rhetoric adopted by the mainstream political parties. Wyn Jones (2001) noted, for example, that Plaid Cymru took the symbolic step in adopting a bilingual name 'Plaid Cymru – The Party of Wales' in 1998 and the Labour Party, under Rhodri Morgan, rebranded itself as 'Welsh Labour' and adopted the rhetoric of 'clear red water' in order to distance themselves from the New Labour government at Westminster. Therefore, the changing nature of the political and electoral landscape within Wales potentially had far-reaching consequences for policy in the post-devolved context, notably driving policy divergence from the UK government in a wide range of areas such as education and health.

The changing political landscape within Wales can also be seen to greater and lesser degrees at the general and local elections which have taken place since the introduction of devolution. In the UK-wide general elections, the gradual shift in support away from the Labour Party, primarily towards the Conservatives, reflected a similar pattern across the UK (Denver, 2010). In the 2005 and 2010 elections, key UK-wide factors such as the opposition to the Iraq war, the emerging economic crisis and the negative perceptions of Gordon Brown's leadership led to a major slump in the Labour Party's vote from the high watermark of 1997 (Johnston and Pattie, 2011; Kavanagh and Cowley, 2010; Kavanagh and Butler, 2005). However, Bradbury (2010: 729–31) argues that, in the Welsh context, the 2010 General Election was, on the one hand, a bad night – representing the party's worst vote share performance in a UK election in Wales since 1918 – but, on the other hand, the party's dominance was maintained, partly due to the disproportionate nature of the electoral system – with the party winning 65 per cent of the seats in Wales on 36.2 per cent of the votes (see Table 2.4). Furthermore, he argues that the election result reflected the emerging multi-level electoral politics following devolution, with a clear pattern of Plaid Cymru performing considerably better in Assembly elections – at least prior to 2011 – but failing to make any significant headway in Westminster elections (see Table 2.3 and Table 2.4). The creation of these multi-level dynamics within

Table 2.3 National Assembly for Wales election results, 2003–11

	Cons	Lab	Lib Dem	Plaid	Other	Total
2003 Assembly election						
Constituency seats	1	30	3	5	1	40
Regional seats	10	0	3	7	0	20
Total seats won	11	30	6	12	1	60
Change	2	2	0	−5	1	−
Constituency ballot						
Votes (000s)	169	341	120	180	40	850
Share of vote %	19.9	40	14.1	21.2	4.7	100
Change %	4.1	2.4	0.7	−7.2	0	−
Regional ballot						
Votes (000s)	163	311	108	168	101	850
Share of vote %	19.2	36.6	12.7	19.7	11.9	100
Change %	2.7	1.2	0.2	−10.8	6.7	−
2007 Assembly election						
Constituency seats	5	24	3	7	1	40
Regional seats	7	2	6	8	0	20
Total seats won	12	26	9	15	1	60
Change	1	−4	0	3	0	−
Constituency ballot						
Votes (000s)	219	315	144	219	81	978
Share of vote %	22.4	32.2	14.8	22.4	8.3	100
Change %	2.4	−7.8	0.6	1.2	3.5	−
Regional ballot						
Votes (000s)	209	289	115	205	157	975
Share of vote %	21.5	29.6	11.7	21	16.1	100
Change %	2.3	−6.9	−1	1.3	4.3	−
2011 Assembly election						
Constituency seats	6	28	1	5	0	40
Regional seats	8	2	4	6	0	20
Total seats won	14	30	5	11	0	60
Change	2	4	−1	−4	−1	−
Constituency ballot						
Votes (000s)	237	402	100	183	27	949
Share of vote %	25	42.3	10.6	19.3	2.8	100
Change %	2.6	10.1	−4.2	−3.1	−5.4	−
Regional ballot						
Votes (000s)	214	350	76	170	139	949
Share of vote %	22.5	36.9	8	17.9	14.7	100
Change %	1.1	7.2	−3.7	−3.1	−1.5	−

Source: House of Commons (2003); National Assembly for Wales (2007, 2011b).

electoral politics raises key questions as to the extent to which voters differentiate between elections and the respective responses of sub-state and state-wide political parties (Hough and Jeffery, 2006).

Perhaps a more significant shift in terms of the impact of devolution and multilevel dynamics on electoral politics within Wales has been the major shifts in the

Table 2.4 Mainstream political parties' performance in general elections, 1997–2011 (total of 40 seats)

	*1997**	*2001**	*2005**	*2010**
Conservatives				
Number of seats (change)	0	0 (0)	3 (+3)	8 (+5)
Share of votes (change) %	19.6	21.0 (+1.5)	21.4 (+0.4)	26.1 (+4.7)
Number of votes	317,145	288,665	297,830	382,730
Labour				
Number of seats (change)	34	34 (0)	29 (−5)	26 (−3)
Share of votes (change) %	54.7	48.6 (−6.1)	42.7 (−5.9)	36.2 (−6.5)
Number of votes	886,935	666,956	594,821	531,601
Liberal Democrats				
Number of seats (change)	2	2 (0)	4 (+2)	3 (−1)
Share of votes (change) %	12.3	13.8 (1.5)	18.4 (+4.6)	20.1 (+1.7)
Number of votes	200,020	189,434	256,249	295,164
Plaid Cymru				
Number of seats (change)	4	4 (0)	3 (−1)	3 (0)
Share of votes (change) %	9.9	14.3 (14.4)	12.6 (−1.7)	11.3 (−1.3)
Number of votes	161,030	195,893	174,838	165,394

Source: House of Commons (2001a, 2001b, 2005, 2011).

*Turnout 1999 – 73.5%; 2001 – 61.6%; 2005 – 62.6%; 2010 – 64.9%.

fortunes of the major political parties at local elections. Morgan and Mungham (2000: 76) note that Labour's hegemony within Wales was first established in the world of local government and that 'for the best part of the twentieth century the Labour Party has dominated town halls and county halls throughout Wales and, in most authorities in the Valleys, it has held unbroken office the whole time'. The Labour Party's hegemony at the local level was challenged prior to devolution; for example, in 1976 Labour lost control of all but 12 of the 37 district councils (Tanner, 2000). By the mid-1990s the Labour Party had re-established itself as the primary party of local government in Wales securing 14 of the 22 newly formed unitary authorities and 43.6 per cent of the votes in the 1995 local elections. Over the course of local elections in 1999, 2003 and 2008 the Labour Party lost more than half of its council seats and remained in control of just two councils (see Table 2.5). This decline can be partly attributed to the usual effects of mid-term elections on a sitting government and was, once again, replicated across the UK (Rallings and Thrasher, 2008). However, the potential impact of this shift in local electoral politics on the policy landscape within Wales should not be under-estimated. From 2004, for example, the Welsh Local Government Association (WLGA), the representative organisation for local authorities, adopted cross-party power-sharing arrangements and, from 2008, was led by Councillor John Davies, leader of Pembrokeshire County Council, on behalf of the Independent group, the Association's largest political group. Notably, party political incongru-ence between the devolved and local level potentially provides one source of tension in the future of local–central relations within a devolved context.

Table 2.5 Mainstream political parties' and independents' performance in local elections, 1995–2008 (total of 22 councils)

	1995	1999	2004	2008
Conservatives				
Number of councils controlled (change)	0	0 (0)	1 (+1)	2 (+1)
Number of seats won	42	75	107	174
Share of seats (change) %	3.3	5.9 (+2.6)	8.5 (+2.6)	13.8 (+5.3)
Share of the vote won (change) %	8.1	10.1 (+2.0)	11.0 (+2.6)	15.6 (+4.6)
Labour				
Number of councils controlled (change)	14	8 (–6)	8 (0)	2 (–6)
Number of seats won	726	563	479	345
Share of seats (change) %	57.1	44.3 (–12.8)	37.9 (–6.4)	27.3 (–10.6)
Share of the vote won (change) %	43.6	34.4 (–9.2)	30.6 (–3.8)	26.6 (–4.0)
Liberal Democrats				
Number of councils controlled (change)	0	0 (0)	0 (0)	0 (0)
Number of seats won	79	98	146	166
Share of seats (change) %	6.2	7.7 (+1.5)	11.6 (+3.9)	13.1 (+1.5)
Share of the vote won (change) %	10.2	13.4 (+3.2)	13.9 (+0.5)	12.9 (–1.0)
Plaid Cymru				
Number of councils controlled (change)	1	3 (+2)	1 (–2)	0 (–1)
Number of seats won	113	205	175	205
Share of seats (change) %	8.9	16.1 (+7.2)	13.8 (–2.3)	16.2 (+2.4)
Share of the vote won (change) %	12.5	18.2 (+5.7)	16.4 (–1.8)	16.9 (+0.5)
Independents				
Number of councils controlled (change)	4	3 (–1)	3 (0)	4 (+1)
Number of seats won	292	295	322	346
Share of seats (change) %	23	23.2 (+0.2)	25.5 (+2.3)	27.4 (+1.9)

Source: National Assembly for Wales (2008).

Building a partnership of equals? Central–local relations in Wales

The introduction of devolved administrations across the UK has been characterised as establishing 'a new set of intergovernmental relations at the regional level' centred on the creation of new 'centres' in Belfast, Cardiff and Edinburgh (Laffin et al., 2000: 223). Conventional wisdom has argued that a strong intermediate layer of devolved government and strong local governments are incompatible and that a process of regionalisation tends to lead to 'regional centralism' or a 'decentralisation of centralism', whereby newly established devolved administrations grasp or suck-up powers from the local governments within their jurisdictions (Laffin, 2004; Jeffery, 1998). However, Jeffrey (2006: 58) noted that, in the UK context, the erosion of local government functions driven by the Conservative governments between 1979 and 1997 had created 'a lingering atmosphere of distrust and tension in central–local relations' and that this experience, combined with the perceived potential benefits of devolution in terms of enhanced access and influence over decision-making, led to a sense that 'things can only get better'. Furthermore, in the Welsh context this optimism was enhanced by the commitment to protect the role of local government emphasised by the UK Government's White Paper *A Voice for Wales* and the rhetoric of 'partnership' and 'inclusivity' adopted by the then Secretary of State for Wales, Ron Davies (HM Government, 1997; Chaney and Fevre, 2001). Laffin et al. (2002: 4) argued that this commitment reflected less a 'thought-out blueprint of post-devolution central–local relations' and more the pragmatic need to secure local government support in the pre-legislative referendum in September 1997. However, the extent to which the rhetoric of partnership has been reflected in the reality of central–local relations following the introduction of devolution remains open to question.

The initial analysis of post-devolution central–local relations in Scotland and Wales suggested that the discretion and autonomy of individual local authorities had increased or been maintained at pre-devolution levels and that the collective influence of local government on the newly devolved centres had significantly increased (Bennett et al., 2002; Laffin et al., 2002). Indeed, a common feature of central–local relations across the UK since devolution has been the emphasis placed on the language of 'partnership' between different levels of government. In the Welsh context, for example, Entwistle (2006: 234–5) noted that the notion of partnership has been 'inextricably bound up with the development of the new, devolved institutions of government in Wales' and has been 'at the heart of the Assembly Government's policy style'. The early rhetoric from senior politicians stressed that the relationship between the Assembly and local government reflected a 'partnership of equals' and was one of the 'golden threads of partnership' at the heart of devolution (Essex, 1998; Michael, 1999). This commitment to enabling local government to 'flourish' was a key tenet of *A Voice for Wales* and was built into the Government of Wales Act 1998 via the Local Government Partnership Scheme and Partnership Council (HM Government, 1997). In practice, the operation of the Partnership Council has been characterised as providing a 'necessary symbolism' for the conduct of Assembly–local government relations, with the core processes of central–local relations taking place through less formal channels (Thomas, 2002: 46).

The overall character of central–local relations in Wales following devolution can be seen as being shaped by several overarching sets of drivers. First, the relatively small size of the Welsh polity, combined with the institutional character of local government within Wales following the creation of a single tier of 22 unitary authorities via the 1996 reorganisation, has facilitated much closer relations between the local level and the newly devolved centre. Entwistle (2006: 232) argued that 'the small size of Welsh polity' facilitated different patterns of partnership working in comparison to elsewhere in the UK and provided 'much stronger vertical links between practitioners on the ground and officials and Ministers in Cardiff'. Although the 'closeness' of Wales may provide a setting where 'everyone knows everyone else', it is crucial not to confuse levels of access and dialogue with political clout (Wilson, 2003). Second, the perceived lack of policy-making capacity inherited by the Assembly administration from the Welsh Office forced Assembly Ministers and officials to draw on the expertise of public sector professionals within local authorities and the WLGA. Laffin (2004: 220) argued that the impact of this 'policy development deficit' was that the 'Assembly is much more dependent on local government than the Westminster government is on English local government'. Entwistle (2006: 233) notes that this relatively high level of power dependency has shaped the policy-making process in Wales and 'given rise to relatively tight policy communities, which in turn favour partnership solutions'. Finally, for much of the early period of the Assembly, Labour Party channels and solidarity were seen as the 'political glue' which held central–local relations together and supplemented the more formal institutional arrangements (Rawlings, 2003: 337). However, as noted in the previous section, the changing nature of the political and electoral landscape within Wales has meant that central–local relations within Wales can no longer be understood simply as an internal Labour Party issue.

Since the introduction of devolution, a key focus for debates on central–local relations within Wales has centred on the 'marriage of necessity' between the Assembly and local government in terms of the delivery of policy and public services on the ground (Essex, 1998). The Welsh government's approach to monitoring service delivery has been characterised as rejecting the market-driven, centralist approach adopted by New Labour at the UK level and instead centred on a positive view of local government based on the recognition of its commitment and capacity to drive improvement from the bottom up (Andrews and Martin, 2010). Laffin (2004: 217–20) notes that, while this alternative approach to central–local relations explicitly rejected the 'naming and shaming' approach adopted by New Labour in England, there was a clear recognition by both Assembly Ministers and local government leaders that 'if local authorities fail to raise their performance, the Welsh government may feel compelled to take a more interventionist approach.' Furthermore, a recurring issue which has framed central–local relations and the delivery of public services has been question marks regarding the effectiveness of the local government model introduced in 1996 in responding to the key policy challenges facing contemporary Wales (see Figure 2.1). In July 2011, for example, the Welsh Government argued that the creation of the relatively small 22 unitary authorities created a range of challenges related to 'patchy performance, leadership, critical mass, specialist expertise, and efficiency' (Welsh Government, 2011a). Therefore the Welsh Government has faced the challenge of responding to the potential problems created by the sub-optimal structure of local government in Wales, while retaining its commitment to partnership.

The Welsh Government's response to these issues, outlined within *Making the Connections* (Welsh Assembly Government, 2004a), stressed the importance of promoting a more integrated approach to public service delivery via the coordination of agencies, goals and collaboration across functional and organisational

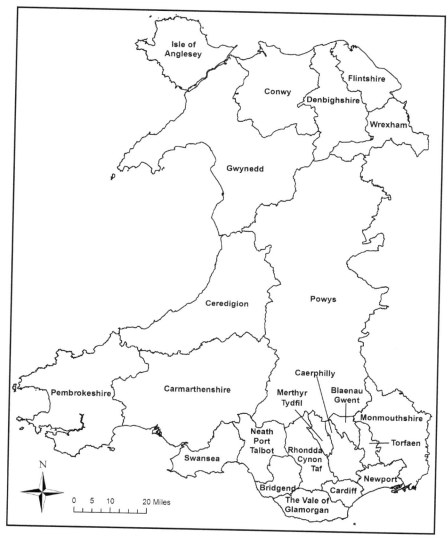

Figure 2.1 Twenty-two unitary authorities post-1996 local government reorganisation

Source: Office of National Statistics, 1996.
Contains Ordnance Survey data © Crown copyright and database right 2012.

boundaries (Martin et al., 2011). This approach was further underpinned by the findings of the independent Beecham Review (Welsh Assembly Government, 2006a) which argued that collaboration and citizen engagement needed to go further in responding to the complexity of governance arrangements and the engrained 'silo mentality' of key policy actors. The Welsh government's commitment to promote integration, coordination and collaboration between local, regional and national public sector organisations in delivering public services was highlighted by the creation of Local Service Boards and Agreements (Welsh Assembly Government, 2006b, 2007a). However, a review of the Welsh Government's approach to local government carried out by Martin et al. (2011) noted that, although such initiatives had improved collaboration and understanding between actors engaged in service delivery, the level of performance across Wales was patchy, partnership arrangements had been slow to bed down and there was little evidence of them delivering geographies or economies of scale. Furthermore, Martin et al. (2011: 100) argued that six years on from Beecham there were still difficulties created by 'the multitude of overlapping regional, sub-regional and local structures' and that there was a risk that these structures could create confusion, wasteful duplication and undermine lines of accountability.

In September 2010, the Local Government Minister, Carl Sargeant, commissioned an independent review of the delivery of public services provided by the 22 local authorities. The review, led by Joe Simpson from the Local Government Leadership Centre, explored many of the issues highlighted by previous reviews, such as the complexity and overlapping nature of governance arrangements (Welsh Government, 2011a). A key principle that underpinned the review's interim report, published in March 2011, was that the creation of a 'one-size-fits-all', standardised administrative geography was inappropriate for the delivery of local authority services. The Welsh Government's response to the Simpson Review argued that while existing initiatives and collaborations should not necessarily be 'unpicked', the variable approach to collaboration and, by implication, the varying construction of regions and sub-regions across policy fields was 'too complex to provide the governance and accountability required in order to move from collaboration to integrated joint service delivery' (Welsh Government, 2011b: 2). The Welsh Government argued that a common set of geographical boundaries and regional arrangements would facilitate delivery by enhancing a range of factors, including clarity of intent, accountability, stability of arrangements and policy-making capacity. The Welsh Government suggested that a structure of six regions, based on the existing Local Health Board boundaries, should be established to provide viable collaborative delivery units, with broad demographic coherence and critical mass (see Figure 2.2). These proposals recognised that the strategic benefits of standardised regions needed to be balanced against a number of risks, including the potential for cross-boundary working to be undermined by the hardening of regional boundaries (Welsh Government, 2011b). The six standardised regions put forward by the Welsh Government are not unproblematic and, unsurprisingly, the local authorities and WLGA initially opposed them. The regional boundaries cut across historical legacies of partnership working, notably in south Wales, and are not conterminous with the regions identified by the Welsh government's key strategic plan, the Wales Spatial Plan. Therefore, the introduction of a standardised regional tier for the delivery of public services, as noted in Chapter 1, potentially significantly reshapes not only the character of central–local relations, but also the strategic and the policy landscape within Wales.

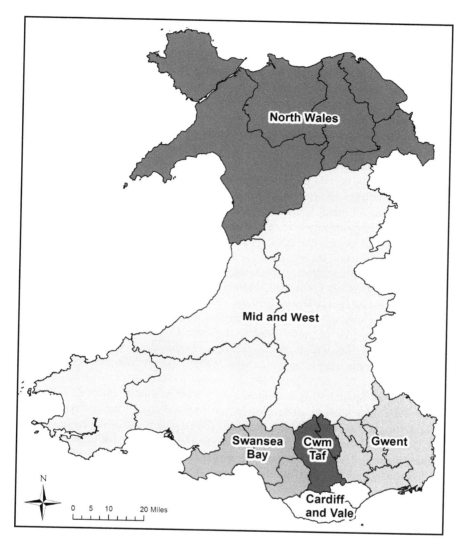

Figure 2.2 Welsh government's proposed alignment of collaborative organisational groups

Source: Welsh Government (2011b).
Contains Ordnance Survey data © Crown copyright and database right 2012.

Developing a strategic vision for Wales: the Wales Spatial Plan

A recurring feature of the policy landscape in Wales since the introduction of devolution has been the attempt by the devolved administration to provide a long-term strategic vision or plan which would effectively join up strategies across a wide range of policy fields. The politically chaotic nature of the National Assembly's first term meant that several overarching policy documents were published within the space of 18 months. First, *BetterWales.com*, was published in May 2000, just a few months following Alun Michael's resignation as First Secretary (National Assembly for Wales, 2000). The strategy provided an overview of the long-term vision for Wales, set out the key tenets of a distinctive 'Made in Wales' approach to policy-making and identified the three overarching themes which shaped the Assembly's wider policy agenda: sustainable development; tackling social disadvantage; and equal opportunities. Second, the partnership agreement between the Welsh Labour Party and Welsh Liberal Democrats, *Putting Wales First: A Partnership for the People of Wales*, published in October 2000, adopted the central themes identified by *BetterWales.com*, but put forward reframed principles and initiatives across a range of policy areas (Wales Labour Party and Welsh Liberal Democrats, 2000). Finally, these guiding principles and programme for government were restated in the strategic plan, *Plan for Wales 2001*, published in October 2001 (National Assembly for Wales, 2001a). These various policy documents provided the high-level context for strategies emerging within specific policy fields – for example, the education and lifelong strategy, *The Learning Country* (National Assembly for Wales, 2001b) and the economic development strategy, *A Winning Wales* (National Assembly for Wales, 2001c). Although the publication of strategic plans became a standard feature of each new Assembly term (for example, *Wales: A Better Country* was published at the beginning of the second Assembly term), a notable development has been the influential role played by the Wales Spatial Plan (Welsh Assembly Government, 2003a).

The Wales Spatial Plan was rooted in the commitment outlined within the *BetterWales.com* strategy to develop 'a new national spatial framework for planning, setting a clear context for sustainable development and environmental quality' (National Assembly for Wales, 2000: 3). Harris (2006: 100) noted that this commitment to developing a national spatial framework provided 'the potential to help tailor policies and develop actions that are appropriate to each of the different parts of Wales'. Furthermore, Harris and Hooper (2006: 141) argue that the process of developing the Welsh Spatial Plan 'transformed a physical space into an explicitly political space' and challenged the 'one-size-fits-all' approach to policy-making which had assumed the functional coherence of Wales as a region. The final Wales Spatial Plan was published in November 2004, following an extensive consultation process around a draft plan published in September 2003 (Welsh Assembly Government, 2003b, 2004b). Haughton et al. (2010: 140–1) note that the approach to consultation was 'an integral and important part of the plan process' and was 'deliberately structured to get a wider range of sectors and stakeholders engaged than is typical for planning strategies'. Furthermore, they argue that this approach meant that rather than simply duplicating approaches to spatial planning adopted elsewhere, there was a sense that 'many of the key policies of the WSP [Wales Spatial Plan] are expected to emerge organically through debate and being tested against local stakeholder opinion rather than developed first by a cadre of professional planners'. Therefore, the shape and focus of this Wales Spatial Plan was very much up for grabs. Harris (2006: 99) noted, for example, that the proposed framework was initially welcomed by the planning community, who saw it as 'a potential solution to the limited strategic planning capacity that existed in Wales following the reorganisation of local government in 1996'. However, rather than providing a focus for traditional statutory planning and land-use planning processes, the Wales Spatial Plan which emerged in 2004 was designed to act primarily as a tool for improving policy-making and integration, while recognising the distinctiveness of different localities within Wales (Harris and Hooper, 2003).

The final version of the Wales Spatial Plan identified two key roles for the plan within the wider devolved policy landscape (Welsh Assembly Government, 2004b: 4):

1. To ensure the Welsh Assembly Government and its partners and agents develop policy in ways which take account of the different challenges and opportunities in the different parts of Wales; and
2. To provide a basis and momentum for working together on a shared agenda locally, so that the different parts of Wales can establish their own distinctive approaches to meet the objectives set in the strategic plan *Wales: A Better Country* and the Assembly's Sustainable Development Scheme.

Furthermore, the Welsh Assembly Government argued that the plan would be 'embedded' in central policy processes and therefore deliver a number of functions, including the provision of 'a clear framework for future collaborative action involving the Welsh Assembly Government and its agencies, local authorities, the private and voluntary sectors to achieve the priorities it sets out nationally and regionally' (Welsh Assembly Government, 2004b: 4). Harris and Hooper (2006: 139) note that the focus of the primary aims and objectives identified by the Welsh Assembly Government mean that 'the objective of policy integration dominates the plan'. Similarly, Haughton et al. (2010: 133) argue that the use of the plan as a source of high-level guidance to guide future development, rather than providing detailed allocations in areas like housing growth and investment, reflects a distinctive 'Welsh approach' to spatial planning.

This 'Welsh approach' was reflected in the key features of the Wales Spatial Plan and, in particular, the creation of areas or sub-regions which were non-conterminous with existing local authority or other sub-national administrative boundaries and the use of 'fuzzy boundaries' to define these areas. The consultation draft plan proposed a combination of loosely defined zones and areas which cut across functional, political and cultural boundaries (but these proved problematic and were replaced in the final plan by six areas) (Harris and Hooper, 2006). In addition, the 'national vision' of Wales outlined within the 2008 Update provided greater detail on key settlements central to the region's development, cross-boundary settlements, socio-economic hubs and international, interregional and regional links. The Wales Spatial Plan set out a range of objectives and actions focused on five core themes: building sustainable communities, promoting a sustainable economy, valuing our environment, achieving sustainable accessibility and respecting distinctiveness. These themes were then considered within the specific context of each of the Spatial Plan areas; for example, in the 2008 Update the discussion of 'promoting a sustainable economy' within the largely rural central Wales area focused primarily on agriculture and tourism, but also identified the importance of supporting micro and social enterprises and providing adequate ICT infrastructure (Welsh Assembly Government, 2008: 59–62). However, it is important to stress that the discussion of these themes remained at a strategic level rather than providing a well-defined budgeted and timetabled programme of actions or schemes.

Since its publication, the role and influence of the Wales Spatial Plan within the wider policy landscape in Wales has been questioned. Perhaps the most common criticism of the Plan has been its relative lack of detailed information on implementation and the generality of its language and commitments (Harris and Hooper, 2006; Osmond, 2006; Haughton et al., 2010). Harris (2006: 102) argues, for example, that the Wales Spatial Plan 'cannot accurately be described as a plan, but is perhaps best understood as a general framework for future collaborative work or, in its own words, it establishes "a direction of travel"'. Haughton et al. (2010: 144) note that four principal concerns were highlighted by the consultation process around the 2008 Update: i) the perception that the main impact had been on 'governmental processes' rather than 'implementation on the ground'; ii) the Plan's level of generality had provided consensus 'at the expense of not setting out distinctive policies that will find their way through to implementation'; iii) the relative weakness of the evidence base; and iv) the primary focus on economic development at the expense of sustainable development. Furthermore, some of the more innovative aspects of the Wales Spatial Plan have proven problematic to implement in practice. Haughton et al. (2010: 146) note that the use of 'fuzzy boundaries' caused 'initial consternation among local authorities' and a potential lack of transparency and accountability, particularly in areas where authorities may find themselves in multiple Spatial Plan Areas. However, they go on to state that these boundaries became 'slightly less fuzzy in practice' and that the need to provide statistical data for Spatial Plan areas had driven a 'firming up' of boundaries around pre-existing administrative areas (Welsh Assembly Government, 2007b).

Despite the potential deficiencies of the Wales Spatial Plan identified by its critics, it is important not to underestimate the level of influence that it has had in reshaping the wider strategic policy context within Wales and driving attempts to deliver policy integration. Harris (2006: 102) argues, for example, that the Plan's 'real value is in having established a reasonably broad consensus on the particular challenges facing the different parts of Wales, suggesting the future role that the different regions may play and identifying a limited series of actions that can be taken to progress in that direction'. The key to unlocking the debates around the value and effectiveness of the Wales Spatial Plan rests on understanding the original role of the Plan envisaged by the Welsh Assembly Government. Haughton et al (2010: 143) note that, on the one hand, 'those who are most vocally in opposition frequently want it [the Wales Spatial Plan] to be something other than what it has set out to be and, unsurprisingly, it is found wanting'. Alternatively, on the other hand, 'those who support it tend to be those who take the Wales Spatial Plan on its own terms, as an ongoing process for brokering agreement in the context of a new territorial government which needed to build consensus rather than impose a particular political agenda for development'. The extent to which the Plan has facilitated policy integration at both the national and sub-regional level and tied into the specific social and economic policy challenges facing different localities within Wales is explored in more depth within the three locality-based chapters later in this volume.

Conclusions

The argument that the introduction of devolution has fundamentally recast the policy landscape within Wales is unquestionable. This chapter has explored four key elements of this changing landscape: the changing nature of the institutional character of devolved governance within Wales, the reshaping of the political and electoral identity of Wales since devolution, the evolving shape of intergovernmental relations between the local and newly devolved 'centre' and, finally, the strategic policy context which has framed attempts to develop a spatially sensitive approach to policy integration across Wales. However, it is important to note that these elements have had varying impacts across different policy areas. The Assembly's substantial powers within health and education policy, for example, have driven a distinctively 'Welsh' policy agenda and led to a significant divergence or 'clear red water' from the policy direction pursued elsewhere in the UK, particularly England (Greer, 2004; Rees, 2007; Davies and Williams, 2009). Similarly, the 'bonfire of the quangos' driven by the Welsh Assembly Government's decision to bring the functions of the WDA, Wales Tourist Board and Education and Learning Wales (ELWa) 'in-house' has been characterised as reflecting a 'state-centric' approach to economic development (Cooke and Clifton, 2005). Although devolution has clearly reshaped the policy landscape within Wales, it is important to note the continued influence of factors whose origins pre-date the introduction of the National Assembly for Wales. Indeed, the policy context across Wales is still highly influenced by many of the interests, identities and institutions inherited from the pre-devolution setting – for example, the continued importance of the language in shaping forms of cultural, political and national identity and the problematic local government structure introduced in 1996. Therefore, in understanding the experiences of the localities across Wales it is important to keep in mind both the forces which have sparked major changes in the policy landscape and those which have driven and continue to drive continuity with the pre-devolution content.

Note

1 Alun Michael, the Assembly's First Secretary between May 1999 and February 2000 had succeeded Ron Davies as Welsh Labour leader following a highly controversial

leadership contest with Rhodri Morgan in early 1999. Following the first Assembly elections he led a minority Labour administration until a vote of no confidence in February 2000. He was succeeded by his former opponent, Rhodri Morgan, who formed a coalition with the Welsh Liberal Democrats in early October 2000. For an insider's account of the leadership election, see Flynn, P. (1999) *Dragons Led By Poodles: The Inside Story of a New Labour Stitch-up* (London: Politicos); and for analysis of Michael's resignation, see Thomas, A. and Laffin, M. (2001) 'The first Welsh constitutional crisis: the Alun Michael resignation', *Public Policy and Administration*, 16(1), 18–31.

References

Aitchison, J. and Carter, H. (2004) *Spreading the Word: The Welsh Language 2001*. Talybont: Y Lolfa.

All Wales Convention (2009) *All Wales Convention Final Report*. Cardiff: NAfW.

Andrews, R. and Martin, S. (2010) 'Regional variations in public service outcomes: the impact of policy divergence in England, Scotland and Wales', *Regional Studies*, 44(8), 919–34.

Balsom, D. (1985) 'The three-Wales model', in Osmond, J. (ed.), *The National Question Again: Political Identity in the 1980s*. Llandysul: Gomer Press. 1–17.

Balsom, D. (2000) 'The first Welsh general election', in Jones, J. B. and Balsom, D. (eds), *The Road to the National Assembly for Wales*. Cardiff: University of Wales Press. 212–28.

Balsom, D., Madgwick, P. and Van Mechelen, D. (1983) 'The red and the green: patterns of partisan choice in Wales', *British Journal of Political Science*, 13, 299–325.

Balsom, D., Madgwick, P. and Van Mechelen, D. (1984) 'The political consequences of Welsh identity', *Ethnic and Racial Studies*, 7, 299–325.

Bennett, M., Fairley, J. and McAteer, M. (2002) *Devolution in Scotland: The Impact on Local Government*. York: Joseph Rowntree Foundation.

Bogdanor, V. (1999) *Devolution in the United Kingdom*. Oxford: Oxford University Press.

Bradbury, J. (1997) 'Conservative governments, Scotland and Wales: a perspective on territorial management', in Bradbury, J. and Mawson, J. (eds), *British Regionalism and Devolution: The Challenges of State Reform and European Integration*. London: Jessica Kingsley. 74–98.

Bradbury, J. (1998) 'The devolution debate in Wales: the politics of a developing union state', in Elcock, H. and Keating, M. (eds), *Remaking the Union: Devolution and British Politics in the 1990s*. London: Frank Cass. 120–39.

Bradbury, J. (2010) 'Wales and the 2010 General Election', *Parliamentary Affairs*, 63(4), 726–41.

Bradbury, J. and Andrews, R. (2010) 'State devolution and national identity: continuity and change in the politics of Welshness and Britishness in Wales', *Parliamentary Affairs*, 63(2), 229–49.

Bradbury, J. and Le Galés, P. (2008) 'Conclusion: UK regional capacity in comparative perspective', in Bradbury, J. (ed.), *Devolution, Regionalism and Regional Development: The UK Experience*. Abingdon: Routledge. 203–17.

Bradbury, J. and Stafford, I. (2008) 'Devolution and public policy in Wales: the case of transport', *Contemporary Wales*, 21, 67–85.

Bradbury, J. and Stafford, I. (2010) 'The effectiveness of legislative mechanisms for the devolution of powers in the UK: the case of transport devolution to Wales', *Public Money and Management*, 30(2), 97–102.

Chaney, P. and Fevre, R. (2001) 'Ron Davies and the cult of inclusiveness: devolution and participation in Wales', *Contemporary Wales*, 14, 21–49.

Chaney, P., Hall, T. and Pithouse, A. (2001) 'New governance – new democracy?', in Chaney, P., Hall, T. and Pithouse, A. (eds), *New Governance – New Democracy? Post-Devolution Wales*. Cardiff: University of Wales Press. 1–17.

Commission on Devolution in Wales (2012) Empowerment and Responsibility: Financial Powers to Strengthen Wales (Cardiff: Commission on Devolution in Wales), 'Commission on Devolution in Wales (2014) Empowerment and Responsibility: Legislative Powers to Strengthen Wales. Cardiff: Commission on Devolution in Wales.

Commission on the Powers and Electoral Arrangements of the National Assembly for Wales (2004) *Report of the Richard Commission*. Cardiff: National Assembly for Wales.

Cooke, P. and Clifton, N. (2005) 'Visionary, precautionary and constrained "varieties of devolution" in the economic governance of the devolved UK territories', *Regional Studies*, 39(4), 437–51.

Coupland, N., Bishop, H. and Garrett, P. (2005) 'One Wales? Reassessing diversity in Welsh ethnolinguistic identification', *Contemporary Wales*, 18, 1–27.

Davies, N. and Williams, D. (2009) *Clear Red Water: Welsh Devolution and Socialist Politics*. London: Fancis Boutle.

Davies, R. (1999) *Devolution: A Process Not an Event*. Cardiff: Institute of Welsh Affairs.

Davies, R. (2005) 'Banal Britishness and reconstituted Welshness: the politics of national identities in Wales', *Contemporary Wales*, 18, 106–21.

Day, G. and Thompson, A. (1999) 'Situating Welshness: "local" experience and national identity', in Fevre, R. and Thompson, A. (eds), *Nation, Identity and Social Theory: Perspectives from Wales*. Cardiff: University of Wales Press.

Deacon, R. M. (2002) *The Governance of Wales: The Welsh Office and the Policy Process 1964–99*. Cardiff: Welsh Academic Press.

Denver, D. (2010) 'The results: how Britain voted', *Parliamentary Affairs*, 63(4), 588–606.

Entwistle, T. (2006) 'The distinctiveness of the Welsh partnership agenda', *International Journal of Public Sector Management*, 19(3), 228–37.

Essex, S. (1998) 'Local government', in Osmond, J. (ed.), *The National Assembly Agenda: A Handbook for the First Four Years*. Cardiff: IWA. 301–7.

Evans, D. (2007) '"How far across the border do you have to be, to be considered Welsh?" – National identification at a regional level', *Contemporary Wales*, 20, 124–43.

Greer, S. (2004) *Territorial Politics and Health Policy: UK Health Policy in Comparative Perspective*. Manchester: Manchester University Press.

Harris, N. (2006) 'Increasing and spreading prosperity: regional development, spatial planning and the enduring 'prosperity gap' in Wales', in Adams, N., Alden, J. and Harris, N. (eds), *Regional Development and Spatial Planning in an enlarged European Union*. Aldershot: Ashgate. 87–106.

Harris, N. and Hooper, A. (2006) 'Redefining "the space that is Wales": place, planning and the Wales Spatial Plan', in Tewdwr-Jones, M. and Allmendinger, P. (eds), *Territory, Identity and Space: Spatial Governance in a Fragmented Nation*. Abingdon: Routledge. 139–52.

Haughton, G., Allmendinger, P., Counsell, D. and Vigar, G. (2010) *The New Spatial Planning: Territorial Management with Soft Spaces and Fuzzy Boundaries*. London: Routledge.

Hill, D., Edwards, H. and Jeffes, L. (2008) *The Evolution of Devolution: Reflections on the Operation of Our Legislative System*. Tredegar: Bevan Foundation.

HM Government (1997) *A Voice for Wales: The Government's Proposals for a Welsh Assembly*, Cm 3718. London: TSO.

HM Government (2006) *The Government of Wales Act 2006*. London: TSO.

HM Government (2015) Powers for a Purpose: Towards a Lasting Devolution Settlement for Wales. London: TSO.

Hough, D. and Jeffery, C. (2006) *Devolution and Electoral Politics*. Manchester: Manchester University Press.

House of Commons (1999) *Welsh Assembly Elections: 6 May 1999*, Research Paper 99/51. London: TSO.

House of Commons (2001a) *General Election results, 1 May 1997*, Research Paper 01/38. London: TSO.

House of Commons (2001b) *General Election results, 7 June 2001*, Research Paper 01/54. London: TSO.

House of Commons (2003) *Welsh Assembly Elections, 1 May 2003*, Research Paper 03/45. London: TSO.

House of Commons (2005) *General Election 2005*, Research Paper 05/33. London: TSO.

House of Commons (2011) *General Election 2010*, Research Paper 10/36. London: TSO.

Housley, W., Smith, R. and Moles, K. (2009) 'Brand, identity or citizenship? The case of post-devolution Wales', *Contemporary Wales*, 22, 196–210.

Jenkins, S. (2014) 'A chance for Wales: can the slumbering dragon awake?', *Guardian*, 30 September, 27–9.

Jeffrey, C. (1998) *Evidence to the Enquiry into the Operation of Multi-Layer Democracy*, Scottish Affairs Committee HC 460–ii. London: HMSO.

Jeffery, C. (2006) 'Devolution and local government', *Publius: The Journal of Federalism*, 36(1), 57–73.

Johnson, N. (2008) 'The Government of Wales Act 2006: Welsh devolution still a process and not an event?', *Web journal of current legal issues*, 2007(4). Available at: http://shura.shu.ac.uk/689/. Accessed: 17 February 2012.

Johnston, R. and Pattie, C. (2011) 'Where did Labour's votes go? Valence politics and campaign effects at the 2010 British General Election', *British Journal of Politics and International Relations*, 13(3), 283–303.

Jones, J. B. (2000) 'Changes to the government of Wales 1979–1997', in Jones, J. B. and Balsom, D. (eds), *The Road to the National Assembly for Wales*. Cardiff: University of Wales Press. 15–27.

Jones, R., Goodwin, M., Jones, M. and Pett, K. (2005) 'Filling in the state: economic governance and the evolution of devolution in Wales', *Environment and Planning C: Government and Policy*, 23(3), 337–60.

Kavanagh, D. and Butler, D. (eds) (2005) *The British General Election of 2005*. Basingstoke: Palgrave Macmillan.

Kavanagh, D. and Cowley, P. (2010) *The British General Election of 2010*. Basingstoke: Palgrave Macmillan.

Laffin, M. (2004) 'Is regional centralism inevitable? The case of the Welsh Assembly', *Regional Studies*, 38(2), 213–23.

Laffin, M., Thomas, A. and Webb, A. (2000) 'Intergovernmental relations after devolution: the National Assembly for Wales', *Political Quarterly*, 71(2), 223–33.

Laffin, M., Taylor, G. and Thomas, A. (2002) *A New Partnership? The National Assembly for Wales and Local Government*. York: Joseph Rowntree Foundation.

Martin, S., Downe, J., Entwistle, T. and Guarneros-Meza, V. (2011) *Learning to Improve: An Independent Assessment of the Welsh Government's Policy for Local Government*, Second Interim Report. Cardiff: WAG.

Michael, A. (1999) *The Dragon on our Doorstep: New Politics for a New Millennium in Wales.* Aberystwyth: Institute of Welsh Politics.

Miers, D. (2011) *Law Making in Wales: A Measure of Devolution,* Paper No. 2. London: The Study of Parliament Group.

Morgan, K. (1997) 'The regional animateur: taking stock of the Welsh development agency', *Regional and Federal Studies,* 7(2), 70–94.

Morgan, K. and Mungham, G. (2000) *Redesigning Democracy: The Making of the Welsh Assembly.* Bridgend: Seren.

Morgan, K. and Roberts, E. (1993) *The Democratic Deficit: A Guide to Quangoland,* Papers in Planning and Research 144. Cardiff: Cardiff University Department of City and Regional Planning.

National Assembly for Wales (2000) *BetterWales.com.* Cardiff: NAfW.

National Assembly for Wales (2001a) *Plan for Wales 2001.* Cardiff: NAfW.

National Assembly for Wales (2001b) *The Learning Country: A Paving Document – A Comprehensive Education and Lifelong Learning Programme to 2010 in Wales.* Cardiff: NafW.

National Assembly for Wales (2001c) *A Winning Wales: The National Economic Development Strategy of the Welsh Assembly Government.* Cardiff: NafW.

National Assembly for Wales (2002) *Assembly Review of Procedure: Final Report.* Cardiff: NAfW.

National Assembly for Wales (2007) *2007 Assembly Election Results* Paper number 07/069. Cardiff: NafW.

National Assembly for Wales (2008) *Local Election Results 2008* Paper number 08/039. Cardiff: NafW.

National Assembly for Wales (2011a) *Results of the National Assembly for Wales Referendum 2011* Paper number 11/017. Cardiff: NAfW.

National Assembly for Wales (2011b) *2011 Assembly Election Results* Paper number 11/023. Cardiff: NAfW.

Navarro, M. and Lambert, D. (2005). *The Nature and Scope of the Legislative Powers of the National Assembly for Wales* Devolution Briefings No. 13. Birmingham: ESRC Devolution Programme.

Navarro, M. and Lambert, D. (2009) Bypassing the Assembly, *Agenda,* Spring, 34–6.

Osmond, J. (2006) *Time to Deliver: The Third Term and Beyond – Policy Options.* Cardiff: Institute of Welsh Affairs.

Pemberton, S. (2000) 'The 1996 reorganization of local government in Wales: issues, process and uneven outcomes', *Contemporary Wales,* 12, 77–106.

Rallings, C. and Thrasher, M. (2008) 'The demise of New Labour? The British 'mid-term' elections of 2008', *Forum,* 6(2), 80–90.

Rawlings, R. (1998) 'The new model Wales', *Journal of Law and Society,* 25(4), 461–509.

Rawlings, R. (2003) *Delineating Wales: Constitutional, Legal and Administrative Aspects of National Devolution.* Cardiff: University of Wales Press.

Rees, G. (2007) 'The impacts of parliamentary devolution on education policy in Wales', *Welsh Journal of Education,* 14(1), 8–20.

Stafford, I. (2011) 'Devolution in Wales and the 2011 Referendum: the beginning of a new era?', *Scottish Affairs,* 77, 28–53.

Tanner, D. (2000) 'Facing the new challenge: Labour and politics 1970–2000', in Tanner, D., Williams, C. and Hopkin, D. (eds), *The Labour Party in Wales 1900–2000.* Cardiff: University of Wales Press. 264–93.

Thomas, A. (2002) 'Realising partnership: relations between the Assembly and local government', in Jones, B. J. and Osmond, J. (eds), *Building a Civic Culture: Institutional Change, Policy Development and Political Dynamics in the National Assembly for Wales*. Cardiff: IWA. 43–55.

Trystan, D., Scully, R. and Wyn Jones, R. (2003) 'Explaining the "quiet earthquake": voting behaviour in the first election to the National Assembly for Wales', *Electoral Studies*, 22, 635–50.

Wales Labour Party and Plaid Cymru (2007) *One Wales: A Progressive Agenda for the Government of Wales*. Cardiff: Wales Labour Party and Plaid Cymru.

Wales Labour Party and Welsh Liberal Democrats (2000) *Putting Wales First: A Partnership for the People of Wales*. Cardiff: Wales Labour Party and Welsh Liberal Democrats.

Wales Office (2005) *Better Governance for Wales*, Cm 6582. London: TSO.

Wales Office (2007) *Wales Office Annual Report 2007*. London: TSO.

Welsh Assembly Government (2003a) *Wales: A Better Country – The Strategic Agenda of the Welsh Assembly Government*. Cardiff: WAG.

Welsh Assembly Government (2003b) *People, Places, Futures: The Wales Spatial Plan – Consultation Draft*. Cardiff: WAG.

Welsh Assembly Government (2004a) *Making the Connections: Delivering Better Services for Wales – the Welsh Assembly Government's Vision for Public Services*. Cardiff: WAG.

Welsh Assembly Government (2004b) *People, Places, Futures: The Wales Spatial Plan*. Cardiff: WAG.

Welsh Assembly Government (2006a) *Beyond Boundaries: Citizen-Centred Local Services for Wales*. Cardiff: WAG.

Welsh Assembly Government (2006b) *Making the Connections – Delivering Beyond Boundaries: Transforming Public Services in Wales*. Cardiff: WAG.

Welsh Assembly Government (2007a) *A Shared Responsibility Local Government's Contribution to Improving People's Lives – A Policy Statement from the Welsh Assembly Government*. Cardiff: WAG.

Welsh Assembly Government (2007b) *Defining the Boundaries of the Wales Spatial Plan Areas for Statistical Data Analysis*. Cardiff: WAG.

Welsh Assembly Government (2008) *People, Places, Futures: The Wales Spatial Plan – 2008 Update*. Cardiff: WAG.

Welsh Government (2011a) *Local, National, Regional: What Services are Best Delivered Where?* Cardiff: Welsh Government.

Welsh Government (2011b) *Public Service Reform: Promoting Regional Coherence – Cabinet Paper (11–12)33*. Cardiff: Welsh Government.

Wigley, D. (2006) *Wales after Richard: Before the 2007 Elections*. Cardiff: Institute of Welsh Affairs.

Williams, J. (2002) 'The Assembly as a legislature', in Jones, J. B. and Osmond, J. (eds), *Building a Civic Culture: Institutional Change, Policy Development and Political Dynamics in the National Assembly for Wales*. Cardiff: Wales Governance Centre and Institute of Welsh Affairs. 1–15.

Wilson, D. (2003) 'Unravelling control freakery: redefining central–local government relations', *British Journal of Politics and International Relations*, 5(3), 317–46.

Wyn Jones, R. (2001) 'On process, events and unintended consequences: national identity and the politics of Welsh devolution', *Scottish Affairs*, 37, 34–57.

Wyn Jones, R. and Lewis, B. (2002) 'The Welsh devolution referendum', *Politics*, 19(1), 37–46.

Wyn Jones, R. and Scully, R. (2003) '"Coming home to Labour"? The 2003 Welsh Assembly Election', *Regional and Federal Studies*, 13(3), 125–32.

Wyn Jones, R. and Scully, R. (2006) 'Devolution and electoral politics in Scotland and Wales', *Publius: The Journal of Federalism*, 36(1), 115–34.

Wyn Jones, R. and Scully, R. (2008) 'The end of one-partyism? Party politics in Wales in the second decade of devolution', *Contemporary Wales*, 21, 207–17.

Wyn Jones, R. and Scully, R. (2012) *Wales Says Yes: The 2011 Welsh Referendum.* Cardiff: University of Wales Press.

3 Wales

A statistical perspective

Samuel Jones, Scott Orford and Gary Higgs

Introduction

Wales is often regarded as being a uniform country, but, as has been highlighted in the previous chapter, it is very diverse with distinct geographical differences in population and other socio-economic and cultural characteristics. This chapter reveals and discusses some of these differences through official statistics presented at a variety of spatial scales with the support of conventional maps, cartograms, graphs and tables. It provides a broad overview of Wales in terms of its demography, its economy and workforce, its mobility in terms of migration and commuting, and issues of identity and the Welsh language. It also highlights how places in Wales can vary in terms of levels of deprivation as measured by official indicators such as the Welsh Index of Multiple Deprivation (WIMD) and by people's attitudes. The discussions are necessarily brief and highlight the main characteristics of each theme. These are then discussed in more detail for particular localities in subsequent chapters, drawing in evidence from key stakeholders and other data. This chapter acts as a precursor to, and a bridge between, this more in-depth exploration of Wales and hence provides a national context to more localised case studies.

A variety of data has been used to provide a broad demographic, socio-economic and cultural overview of Wales. For consistency's sake, and to minimise contradictions between data sources and the stakeholder interviews, all data and analysis relates to either the duration that the study was undertaken (2009–10) or prior to the commencement of the study. Data collected after the end of the study period that has since become available has not been included in the analysis in this chapter. Data that has been used includes Welsh government surveys such as Living in Wales and the WIMD, and UK government surveys such as the Annual Population Survey, the 2001 Census of population and the Annual Survey of Hours and Earnings. As a result, the data varies in the time that it was collected from 2001 for the Census to 2010 for the Annual Population Survey. It also varies in the spatial scale at which it is presented, from Lower Layer Super Output Area (LSOA) for the WIMD, Middle Layer Super Output Area (MSOA) for the demographic data to the unitary authority level for the Annual Population Survey data. This variety in temporal and spatial scales is common in statistical descriptions of the UK and reflects the frequency of surveys, their response rates, protocols relating to statistical disclosure and the conventional units of analysis used in policy research. However, despite variations in the data sources used to construct a picture of the socio-economic geography of Wales, what becomes evident is the strong socio-spatial patterning of the population in relation to these key themes and their relatively consistent and persistent nature over time (e.g. Higgs and White, 1998; Fevre, 1999; Herbert, 1980). These patterns reveal that Wales can be divided into distinct regions, often corresponding to the Wales Spatial Plan areas described in Chapter 2, and it is these regions that are partly investigated in the localities research in the following chapters. A brief overview of patterns of socio-economic conditions in Wales in the early years of the twenty-first century as revealed by these secondary data sources will be presented in the conclusion to this chapter.

Demographics

Wales has a growing but ageing population with its demographic characteristics having a very distinct geography. The majority of the country is sparsely populated with most of the population concentrated in the south east and north east and particularly in the three large cities of Cardiff, Swansea and Newport in the south. The following section draws on secondary data sources to describe the characteristics of the Welsh population in relation to its geography, age structure, demographic composition, country of birth and general health.

Population

Wales had a population of just over 3 million people in 2011 (ONS, 2012). However, the population is not evenly distributed, with large parts of the country being sparsely populated, in particular mid and west Wales, the Welsh border region and the Snowdonia region in north west Wales. Figure 3.1 shows this uneven distribution with population density at the time of the 2001 Census mapped at MSOA level. These are census areas that have a minimum of 5,000 residents and 2,000 households, with a mean population of around 7,200, and adhere to local authority boundaries. Figure 3.1 shows the conventional topographic map of Wales, with MSOAs drawn in proportion to land area. This gives a clear indication of the sparsity of much of central and west Wales, and the concentration of the population into the south east and north east of the country. But by emphasising the sparsely populated rural areas of Wales the map obscures variations in population characteristics in the most densely populated parts of the country that are difficult to discern at this scale of map representation. To address this problem, the map on the right represents the same MSOAs but in this instance the area units have been distorted in proportion to the size of the population living within them. Such a map is called a population cartogram. This 'distorted' map of Wales, with the rural areas of mid and west Wales less prominently displayed and the densely populated areas of south and north east Wales

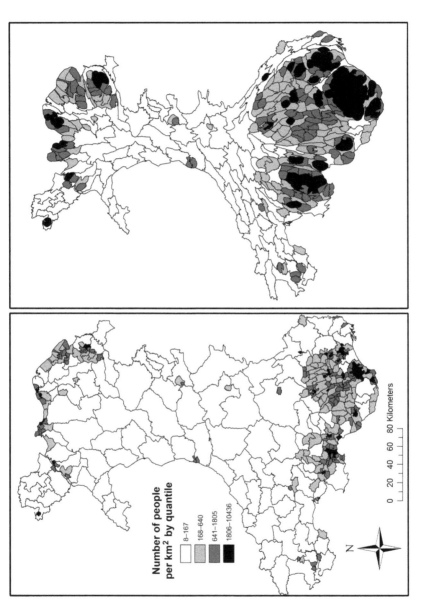

Figure 3.1 Number of people per km² by MSOA

Source: Census 2001.
Contains National Statistics data © Crown copyright and database right 2012.

having been visually exaggerated presents a clearer picture of population trends. Crucially, this distortion is not at the expense of the interpretability of the map with the different parts of Wales being easy to recognise and identify. Hence Cardiff, Swansea and Newport can be seen as three distinct clusters of densely populated areas in the south of the map, with Wrexham clearly identifiable in the north east region of Wales. Smaller urban centres such as Aberystwyth, Rhyl, Llandudno and Bangor also have a larger visual prominence in this map based on population figures than would be displayed on a conventional topographical map. The biggest distinction in the cartogram representation is the size of the Welsh valleys. Together the valleys contain just less than a million people or 30 per cent of the Wales population, but this fact is not immediately visually discernible on a conventional map.

As a general rule, population densities gradually decline when moving with distance away from the urban centres in the south east and north east. Areas in mid and west Wales are sparsely populated with pockets of more densely populated areas around towns such as Holyhead, Newtown, Brecon, Carmarthen, Milford Haven and university towns, such as Aberystwyth and Bangor. Woods (2011) describes how the geography of rural Wales is characterised by the prominence of small market towns and that four out of every ten people in rural Wales live in a small town ranging in size from just under 1,000 people to around 15,000 people. Areas in major transport corridors, such as those of the A55 in the north and the M4 in the south also have higher population densities than areas away from these major highway routes.

Age structure

Figures 3.2 to 3.6 show the proportions of people in different age bands in each MSOA. The map of children age 15 years and younger tends to mirror the map of people aged 25–44, as you would expect given the age structure of most families. There are slightly higher proportions of this age group compared to the 25–44 year age group in general living in the outskirts and suburbs of the major population centres, and some communities in central rural Wales (Woods, 2011). There are higher proportions of 16–24s in areas with universities, such as Pontypridd, Lampeter, Carmarthen, Aberystwyth, Bangor and some of the inner city areas of Cardiff, Newport and Swansea. Higher proportions of this age group are also located in a number of other towns including Brecon, Chepstow, Haverfordwest, Wrexham and locations along the A55 corridor, but there are areas with lower proportions of this age group along the Welsh border and in the sparser rural areas of mid and west Wales and especially historic and coastal towns that are likely to offer limited education and employment opportunities to young people (Woods, 2011). Areas with higher densities of the population in the 25–44-year-old age group are clustered around the major population centres, such as Cardiff, Newport and Wrexham, some communities in the south Wales valleys and along the major transport routes, such as the A55 and, in particular, the M4 corridor. Proportions are lower in areas of mid and west Wales and in some rural

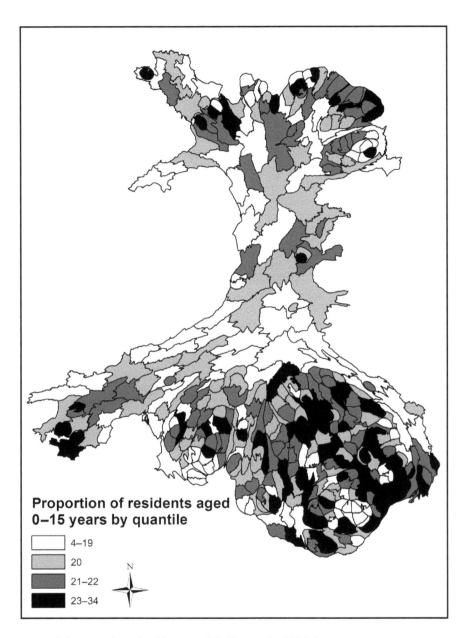

Figure 3.2 Proportion of residents aged 0–15 years by MSOA

Source: Census 2001.
Contains National Statistics data © Crown copyright and database right 2012.
Contains Ordnance Survey data © Crown copyright and database right 2012.

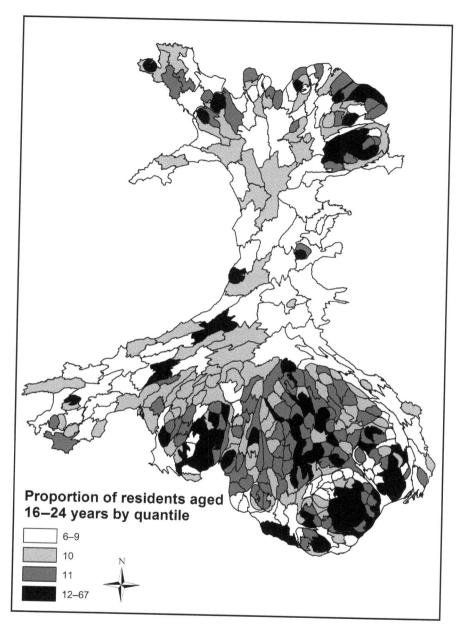

Proportion of residents aged
16–24 years by quantile

	6–9
	10
	11
	12–67

N

Figure 3.3 Proportion of residents aged 16–24 years by MSOA

Source: Census 2001.
Contains National Statistics data © Crown copyright and database right 2012.
Contains Ordnance Survey data © Crown copyright and database right 2012.

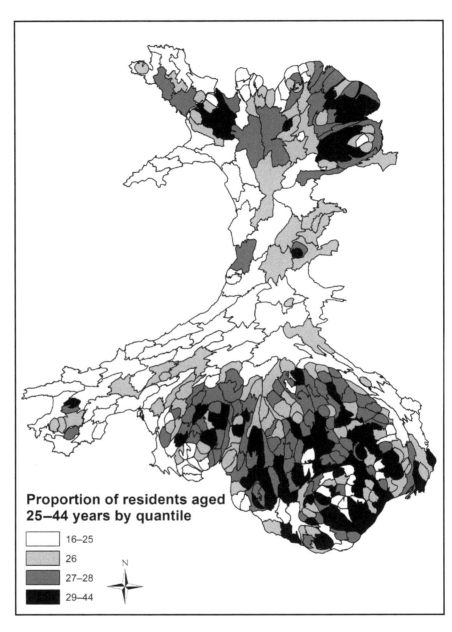

Figure 3.4 Proportion of residents aged 25–44 years by MSOA

Source: Census 2001.
Contains National Statistics data © Crown copyright and database right 2012.
Contains Ordnance Survey data © Crown copyright and database right 2012.

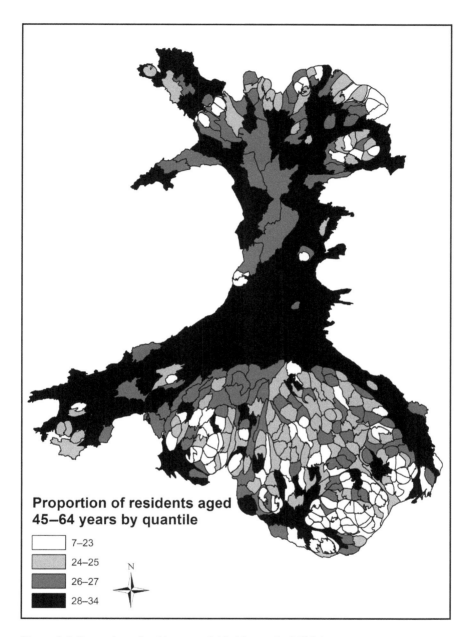

**Proportion of residents aged
45–64 years by quantile**

☐	7–23
▨	24–25
▨	26–27
■	28–34

N

Figure 3.5 Proportion of residents aged 46–64 years by MSOA

Source: Census 2001.
Contains National Statistics data © Crown copyright and database right 2012.
Contains Ordnance Survey data © Crown copyright and database right 2012.

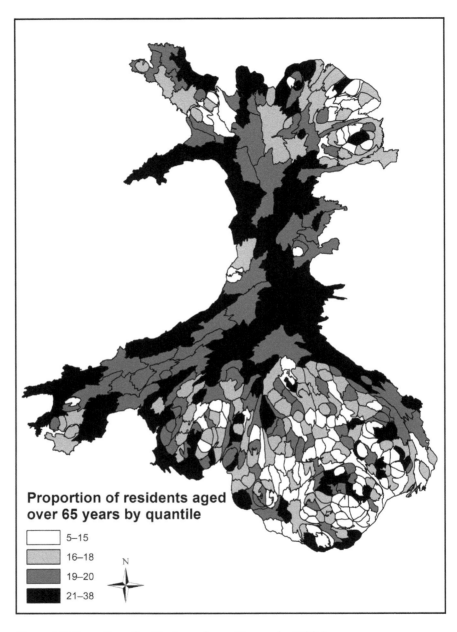

Figure 3.6 Proportion of residents aged over 65 years by MSOA

Source: Census 2001.
Contains National Statistics data © Crown copyright and database right 2012.
Contains Ordnance Survey data © Crown copyright and database right 2012.

communities of south and south east Wales. In contrast, the proportions of 45–64-year-olds appear to be higher outside of the major population centres and the south Wales valleys and, in particular, in the rural areas of mid and west Wales. Even here, the small market towns tend to have smaller proportions of this age group compared to the surrounding rural areas. A similar situation occurs for people aged 65 and over, although they are less concentrated in mid Wales and more concentrated in the retirement areas such as the Llyn Peninsula, areas along the west and north west coastlines, such as Anglesey, Llangollen and Colwyn Bay, and areas such as Tenby, Swansea and the Gower in the south.

Born in Wales

Around three-quarters of the Welsh population were born in Wales (with a further fifth born in England), although this varies quite dramatically across the country as Figure 3.7 clearly shows. The Welsh valleys have very high proportions of their population being born in Wales, a pattern not seen anywhere else in the country. This reflects migration patterns, discussed elsewhere in this chapter (see the section on Migration, below), but essentially fewer people born outside of Wales move into the Welsh valleys compared to other parts of Wales and fewer people born in the Welsh valleys migrate to other parts of the country. The proportions of people born in Wales in North, mid and west Wales are smaller due to the relatively large in-migration of people from outside of the country compared to elsewhere in Wales. There is also a clear border effect due to the use of hospitals in Chester, Shrewsbury and Hereford by prospective mothers who reside in mid and north east Wales. Major population centres, such as Cardiff, Newport, Swansea and Wrexham have lower proportions of their populations born in Wales. Migration to and from these areas is greater, meaning there will be a greater diversity in terms of where people were born.

Long-term limiting illness

Figures from the 2001 Census suggest that 23 per cent of the Welsh population are reported to have a long-term limiting illness compared to 18 per cent for England and the rest of the UK. This is comparable to the situation in the 1991 Census (Senior, 1998). The geography of long-term limiting illness in Wales generally corresponds with patterns of deprivation and also mirrors areas of higher than average numbers of workers previously employed in mining/steel-making. Figure 3.8 shows that areas of the south Wales valleys, particularly the western valleys, have large percentages of people with long-term limiting illnesses as a legacy of mining and heavy industrial activities. Similarly, former coalfield areas of north Wales, particularly along the north east Wales coast, also have high proportions of people with long-term limiting illnesses. In contrast, the proportions of the population with long-term limiting illnesses are lower in rural areas and especially in the affluent rural areas of north east Wales and south and

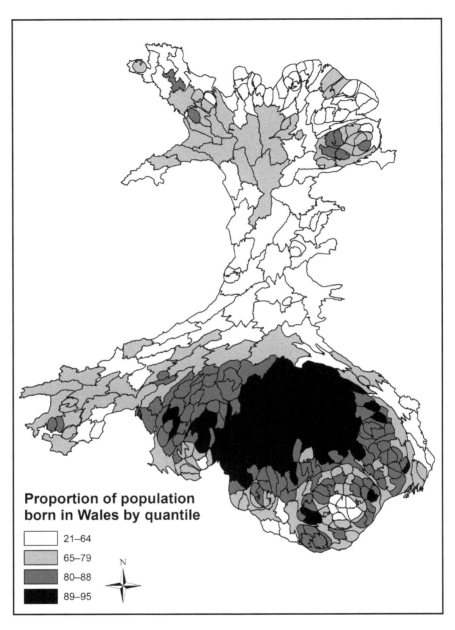

Proportion of population born in Wales by quantile

	21–64
	65–79
	80–88
	89–95

N

Figure 3.7 Proportion of the population who state that they were born in Wales by MSOA

Source: Census 2001.
Contains National Statistics data © Crown copyright and database right 2012.
Contains Ordnance Survey data © Crown copyright and database right 2012.

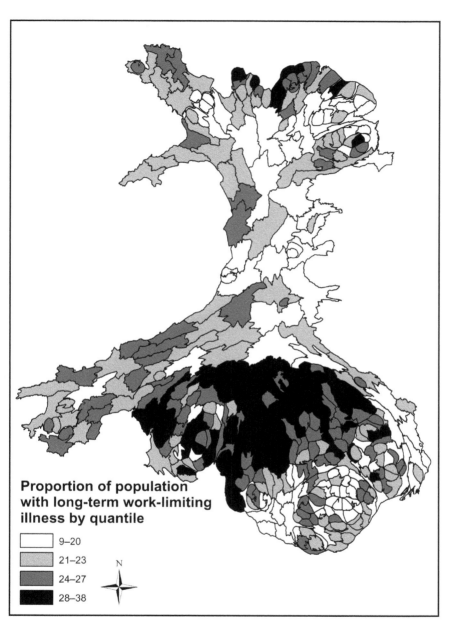

Figure 3.8 Proportion of the population who state that they have a long-term work-limiting illness by MSOA

Source: Census 2001.
Contains National Statistics data © Crown copyright and database right 2012.
Contains Ordnance Survey data © Crown copyright and database right 2012.

south east Wales. However, these are still persistently higher than equivalent areas of limiting long-term illness in the rest of the UK (Senior, 1998).

Lone-parent households

On average 7 per cent of the households in Wales are headed by lone parents (Census 2001). This is slightly higher than the proportions seen in England and the UK as a whole (6.5 per cent). Figure 3.9 shows that the south Wales valley areas have relatively high proportions of lone-parent households, although there are concentrations within local areas of the valleys, which may reflect the provision of social housing. Urban areas also have higher proportions of lone-parent households compared to the rest of Wales. Areas in the north of the country, particularly along the north east coastline, also show higher proportions of lone-parent families. In contrast, there are notably lower proportions of lone-parent households in rural areas of Wales.

Labour market and work force

Wales has a diverse labour market but is more reliant on public sector employment compared to other regions of the UK. The legacy of traditional heavy and extractive industries continues to remain a characteristic of some areas while others are reliant on agriculture and small independent businesses. The M4 and the A55 are important commuting corridors and have concentrations of high-paid professionals and skilled labour. The Welsh valleys, cities and the north east coastal area of Wales have large concentrations of unemployment and benefit claimants. The following section describes the geography of the workforce in Wales in relation to economic activity, occupation structure, skills and qualifications, businesses, wages and claimants.

Economic inactivity

The economic inactivity rate among the working-age population (16–64) in 2010 is higher in Wales than it is for England and the UK as a whole at 27 per cent compared to around 24 per cent (Table 3.1). This is also true for young people between the ages of 16 and 24, although the percentage point difference to the UK is not so great, at only 2 per cent. The unemployment rate in Wales is also higher for the working-age population (8.5 per cent), and the young working-age population (22.5 per cent), than it is for England and the UK as a whole. However, the difference is more marked for young people. Authorities in south west Wales, such as Swansea, Neath Port Talbot, Carmarthenshire and Pembrokeshire, have higher rates than the all-Wales levels of economic inactivity. The authorities of Caerphilly, Blaenau Gwent, Rhondda, Cynon, Taff and Torfaen in the south east valleys also have a higher rate than the all-Wales level. In contrast, economic inactivity rates for the 16–64 age group along the M4 corridor and in mid and north Wales tend to be lower than the all-Wales average.

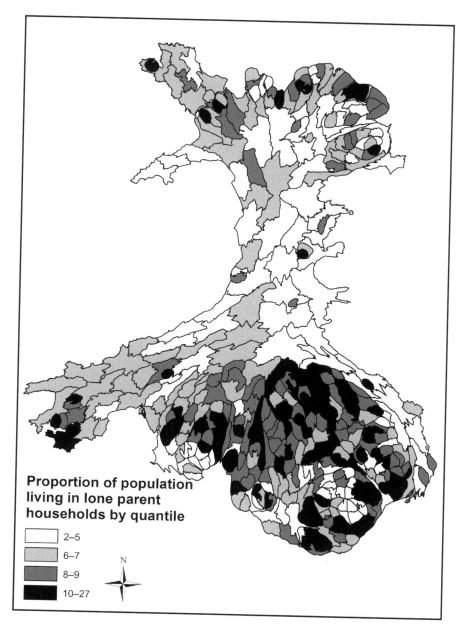

Figure 3.9 Proportion of lone-parent households by MSOA

Source: Census 2001.
Contains National Statistics data © Crown copyright and database right 2012.
Contains Ordnance Survey data © Crown copyright and database right 2012.

Table 3.1 Economic inactivity and unemployment rates by unitary authority

	Economically inactive: 16–64	Economically inactive: 16–24	Unemployment rate: 16–64	Unemployment rate: 16–24
Blaenau Gwent	30.4	29.6	12.7	28.8
Bridgend	25.4	23.6	8.1	25.8
Caerphilly	31.3	37.8	9.4	21.3
Cardiff	27.4	45.4	10.3	27.5
Carmarthenshire	27.7	42.1	8.4	24.8
Ceredigion	26.5	38.4	4.7	11.3
Conwy	27.4	41.8	5.8	13.2
Denbighshire	25.5	33.4	9.2	27.9
Flintshire	22.6	26.3	7.2	18.6
Gwynedd	26.6	44.0	5.9	14.1
Isle of Anglesey	27.1	38.5	4.8	7.0
Merthyr Tydfil	26.6	30.5	11.1	27.2
Monmouthshire	24.9	42.8	5.7	24.9
Neath Port Talbot	32.0	39.8	9.1	27.2
Newport	25.6	33.9	9.9	19.6
Pembrokeshire	27.6	33.3	9.0	22.1
Powys	24.9	35.7	5.7	15.8
Rhondda Cynon Taf	29.4	38.8	11.8	25.5
Swansea	33.3	55.1	8.7	26.0
The Vale of Glamorgan	23.6	35.7	8.4	27.5
Torfaen	28.1	34.8	8.7	20.8
Wrexham	22.1	36.6	6.5	15.3
Wales	27.4	39.5	8.5	22.5
England	23.6	37.5	7.8	19.2
United Kingdom	23.9	37.4	7.8	19.3

Source: Annual Population Survey, 2010.

Flintshire, Blaenau Gwent, Merthyr Tydfil and Bridgend have the lowest economic inactivity rates for the 16–24 year age group other than those areas with large student populations in areas of Cardiff, Swansea, Gwynedd and Ceredigion.

The unemployment rate follows a similar pattern to the economic inactivity rate. Areas in mid and north Wales, with the exception of Denbighshire (which has one of the highest unemployment rates), generally have lower unemployment rates than authorities in the south. The unemployment rate is lower for lesser populated rural areas such as Ceredigion, Powys and Monmouthshire. Areas of south east Wales, particularly the south Wales valley areas (with the exception of Torfaen) and Cardiff, Newport and Neath Port Talbot, have high rates of unemployment. Blaenau Gwent, in the heads of the south Wales valleys, has the highest unemployment rate in Wales. The unemployment rate for young people (16–24) is higher in the south than in mid and north Wales. However, areas in the south Wales valleys, such as Torfaen and Caerphilly, have lower rates than much of the rest of south Wales, as does Newport. The unemployment and economic inactivity rates for all working-age people generally correlate with claimant count

Table 3.2 Percentage of working-age people by formal qualification type by unitary authority

	% of working-age people					
	Degree or equivalent and above	*Higher edu-cation below degree level*	*GCE A level or equivalent*	*GCSE grades A–C or equivalent*	*Other quals*	*No quals*
Blaenau Gwent	10.8	7.9	20.8	28.4	15.6	16.4
Bridgend	19.8	7.7	23.8	25.3	10.5	12.9
Caerphilly	12.9	7.1	20.8	28.4	11.5	19.4
Cardiff	33.6	6.6	19.9	19.2	9.8	10.8
Carmarthenshire	21.9	9.2	21.0	23.2	10.1	14.7
Ceredigion	27.3	9.7	27.6	19.4	8.0	8.1
Conwy	18.5	12.0	18.0	26.5	11.2	13.8
Denbighshire	16.2	10.6	23.1	27.1	10.2	12.9
Flintshire	19.9	9.6	25.4	27.1	8.8	9.1
Gwynedd	19.7	9.6	24.2	24.0	9.0	13.5
Isle of Anglesey	17.9	11.7	26.5	21.9	9.5	12.5
Merthyr Tydfil	12.9	7.5	20.7	27.1	13.0	18.8
Monmouthshire	26.7	10.4	24.2	23.2	6.1	9.4
Neath Port Talbot	11.6	9.9	24.1	27.5	11.0	15.9
Newport	17.5	11.1	21.5	25.3	10.3	14.3
Pembrokeshire	14.8	10.0	24.2	23.2	11.0	16.8
Powys	21.5	9.4	21.3	25.7	10.7	11.4
Rhondda Cynon Taf	14.8	8.1	21.8	25.0	13.4	16.9
Swansea	19.3	8.4	27.7	20.5	9.4	14.7
The Vale of Glamorgan	23.0	9.2	24.6	23.4	10.1	9.7
Torfaen	12.8	10.5	23.8	26.1	11.9	15.0
Wrexham	16.6	8.8	24.0	29.0	11.7	9.8
Wales	19.8	8.9	22.9	24.3	10.5	13.5
England	22.9	8.5	22.1	22.6	12.6	11.2
United Kingdom	22.6	9.0	22.5	22.2	12.0	11.7

Source: Annual Population Survey, 2010.

rates (see section on Claimant count, below). Economic inactivity and unemploy-ment are discussed in more detail in Chapter 4 in relation to the Heads of the Valleys locality.

Qualifications

Of the working-age population in Wales, 14 per cent are found to have no recog-nised qualifications (as compared to 11 per cent for England and the rest of the UK) (Table 3.2). Areas in the south east Wales valleys, Blaenau Gwent (11 per cent), Neath Port Talbot (12 per cent), Torfaen, Caerphilly and Merthyr Tydfil (all at 13 per cent) and Rhondda Cynon Taff (15 per cent) make up six of the seven authorities with the smallest share of residents having a degree (or equivalent) or above. These all fall below the Wales average of 20 per cent. Furthermore, Rhondda Cynon Taff (17 per cent), Merthyr Tydfil (19 per cent) and Caerphilly (19 per cent) make up the areas with the largest share of residents having no recognised formal, or equivalent, qualifications.

The valleys here seem to be in contrast to the majority of the rest of the country. Figure 3.10 shows the percentage of 15-year-olds obtaining five or more A*–C grades at GCSE, or the vocational equivalent of these qualifications in 2010 (GCSE and Equivalent Results in England, Department for Education). The Welsh average lies at 58 per cent, far lower than the average for England for the same year (75 per cent). The south east Wales valleys authorities fall consistently below the Wales average. For the academic year ending in 2010, those achieving five GCSEs A*–C in Merthyr Tydfil, Blaenau Gwent, Torfaen and Rhondda Cynon Taff were in the bottom four, some 4 per cent or more below the Wales average. The Vale of Glamorgan, Ceredigion and Gwynedd were the top performers in terms of students achieving five GCSEs A*–C. Wrexham and Denbighshire, in the north east, also fall below the Wales average, whereas Flintshire is one of the top four. Rural areas of Wales are above the Wales average, with areas in the south east (Cardiff, Bridgend, Monmouth) falling around the average. A more in depth discussion on qualifications can be found in chapters 4, 5 and 6 in relation to the Heads of the Valleys, A55 Corridor and the Central and West Coast localities.

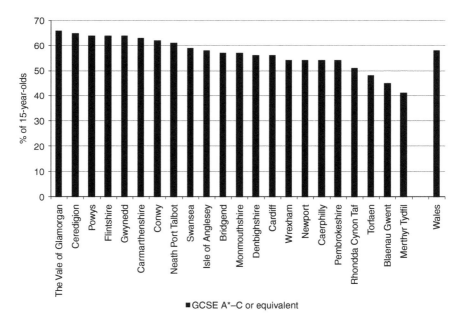

Figure 3.10 Percentage of 15-year-olds attaining 5 GCSEs grades A*–C or vocational equivalent by unitary authority

Source: School Examination Performance Information, Welsh Government, AY 2009–10.

Occupation

Table 3.3 shows the occupation structure in Wales, which approximates to that of the UK as a whole (Annual Population Survey, 2010). In terms of share, Wales has more professional occupations, such as teachers, health professionals, business, media and public service professionals and science and research professionals, than any other category (17.5 per cent), partly reflecting the dominance of the public sector in the country. Jobs as process, plant and machine operatives are the least common at 7.5 per cent, closely followed by customer service and sales at 8.2 per cent. A gender divide exists within some occupation groups. Far more females in Wales are involved in caring, leisure and other service occupations, and sales and customer service occupations, whereas occupations such as process, plant and machine operatives and, particularly, skilled trades are predominantly held by males.

A breakdown of regional patterns in occupational structures within Wales reveals that authorities within the M4 corridor, with the exception of Neath Port

Table 3.3 Share of selected occupation classes by unitary authority

	Managers, directors and senior officials	Professional	Skilled trades	Process, plant and machine operatives	Elementary	Other
Blaenau Gwent	7.7	13.5	11.1	13.6	17.8	35.4
Bridgend	10.1	17.9	10.9	9.8	9.3	41.7
Caerphilly	9.1	12.5	13.6	9.6	10.7	44.0
Cardiff	8.8	25.3	5.5	4.4	7.5	47.5
Carmarthenshire	8.1	21.6	13.8	7.4	10.3	37.9
Ceredigion	9.7	18.6	15.6	3.9	14.1	38.2
Conwy	12.5	17.4	12.6	4.8	10.8	41.3
Denbighshire	9.7	17.3	13.7	6.2	10.8	42.6
Flintshire	9.6	16.0	11.6	9.9	9.4	42.7
Gwynedd	9.3	16.4	15.8	6.5	12.3	39.4
Isle of Anglesey	10.6	15.3	16.5	6.5	10.4	39.9
Merthyr Tydfil	5.5	14.5	13.7	6.3	15.9	42.5
Monmouthshire	11.3	22.5	11.9	5.5	10.3	38.1
Neath Port Talbot	8.3	11.8	14.5	9.8	11.2	44.3
Newport	9.0	15.7	10.5	7.6	14.0	42.8
Pembrokeshire	9.1	12.7	17.1	8.0	13.5	39.2
Powys	13.8	16.5	15.9	7.4	9.7	36.3
Rhondda Cynon Taf	8.4	14.4	12.5	9.1	11.9	42.9
Swansea	7.3	19.5	12.8	7.1	11.5	41.8
The Vale of Glamorgan	11.7	19.3	8.1	4.4	9.8	46.0
Torfaen	9.5	11.5	13.2	8.7	12.6	43.8
Wrexham	8.7	16.7	13.5	11.3	10.2	39.4
Wales	9.4	17.5	12.2	7.5	10.9	41.9
England	10.3	19.0	10.7	6.5	10.7	42.4
United Kingdom	10.0	18.8	11.0	6.6	10.8	42.4

Source: Annual Population Survey, 2010.

Talbot and Newport, have a larger proportion of residents employed in professional occupations, with over a quarter of residents of Cardiff employed in such occupations (the highest in Wales). This is in contrast to the south east valley areas, which are lower than the Welsh average (with Torfaen having the lowest proportion in Wales at 11.5 per cent). Authorities in mid and north Wales fall around the Welsh average, with Flintshire and Wrexham being notably below this value. There are fewer managers, directors and senior officials in the Welsh valleys, and all, with the exception of Torfaen, fall below the Welsh average. Merthyr Tydfil has the lowest proportion of residents employed in these occupations at 5.5 per cent. Residents employed in these occupations are surprisingly few in unitary authorities containing major Welsh urban areas, such as Swansea (7.3 per cent), Wrexham (8.7 per cent), Cardiff (8.8 per cent) and Newport (9 per cent) and have a greater share in rural areas, such as Powys, which has the highest proportion in Wales at 13.8 per cent. This suggests that these areas rely much more on small businesses and could also reflect commuting patterns.

Larger proportions of process, plant and machine operatives can be found in the south east valleys (Blaenau Gwent has the largest proportion in Wales at 13.6 per cent) and in the north east, such as in Wrexham and Flintshire. Merthyr Tydfil and Denbighshire are the exceptions to this. This may be surprising, but when looking at the proportion of industries in Merthyr there are larger numbers of lighter industries, such as retail, and skilled industries, such as construction, than heavier industries such as production. Cardiff and other authorities in the south east, such as the Vale of Glamorgan and Monmouthshire, have few of these operatives. The same is also true for more rural areas in the north and south west of the country, and in mid Wales. Elementary occupations are quite mixed throughout the country, with fewer being found in the east of the country than the west. The south east valley authorities generally have higher proportions of these occupations, with Blaenau Gwent (17.8 per cent) and Merthyr Tydfil (15.9 per cent) having the highest proportions in Wales. The occupations structure in particular parts of Wales and its relationship with education, skills and wages is analysed in more detail in chapters 4 and 6 in relation to the Heads of the Valleys and the Central and West Coast localities.

Business units by size

In Wales the proportions of businesses by size (Table 3.4), as measured by numbers of employees, are very similar to those in England, with around two-thirds of businesses employing four persons or fewer. Less than 10 per cent of businesses in either country employ 20 or more persons. Rural areas, such as Powys, Ceredigion, Carmarthenshire and Monmouthshire, have high proportions of small (0–4 persons) businesses. Fewer of these exist in major cities (such as Swansea, Newport and Cardiff), in unitary authorities in the south east along the M4 corridor and in the valleys areas. Larger businesses of more than 20 persons are prominent in areas such as the south Wales valleys (particularly Merthyr Tydfil and Blaenau Gwent) and along the M4 corridor, and in the north east of

Table 3.4 Business units by number of employees by unitary authority

	Persons employed			
	0–4	*5–9*	*10–19*	*20 or more*
Blaenau Gwent	55.1	20.9	11.1	12.9
Bridgend	59.9	18.5	10.6	11.1
Caerphilly	62.9	17.1	9.1	10.9
Cardiff	59.1	17.5	10.9	12.5
Carmarthenshire	73.6	13.4	7.1	6
Ceredigion	75.5	13.1	7.1	4.3
Conwy	65.6	16.7	9.5	8.2
Denbighshire	65.4	17.2	9.2	8.2
Flintshire	65.2	16	9.3	9.5
Gwynedd	69.7	15.7	8.6	6.1
Isle of Anglesey	70.4	14.7	8.8	6
Merthyr Tydfil	57.6	17.6	11.9	12.9
Monmouthshire	72.8	14.9	6.8	5.5
Neath Port Talbot	60.3	18.1	11.4	10.2
Newport	61	16.6	10.2	12.3
Pembrokeshire	71.2	15.9	7.5	5.5
Powys	77.7	11.8	5.8	4.6
Rhondda Cynon Taf	64.3	16.1	8.7	10.9
Swansea	61.7	17.6	9.8	10.9
The Vale of Glamorgan	68.3	16.4	8.1	7.2
Torfaen	59.2	18.5	10.5	11.8
Wrexham	64.5	16.5	9.3	9.6
Wales	66.6	16.0	8.9	8.6
England	68.2	14.8	8.2	8.8

Source: Inter-Departmental Business Register, 2010.

the country. This reflects the industry types and occupations in the area (see section on Occupation, above).

Wages

In 2010, the gross median wages for full-time workers in Wales were lower than the medians for England and the UK, for both males (£490.10) and females (£405.60), by around £50 per week (Annual Survey of Hours and Earnings, 2010). Full-time female workers in Wales generally earned an average of £84.50 a week less than male workers. The difference here was slightly narrower than in England and the rest of the UK, where the difference was around £100 a week. Figure 3.11 shows the breakdown of wages by unitary authority. Full-time workers living in unitary authorities along the M4 corridor had the highest median weekly wages with workers in the Vale of Glamorgan earning the most (£539.80). Areas within north east Wales on the English border also show higher than average wages, with residents of Flintshire having a median gross weekly wage of £479.10. Rural authorities, such as Powys, Gwynedd and Ceredigion, fall below

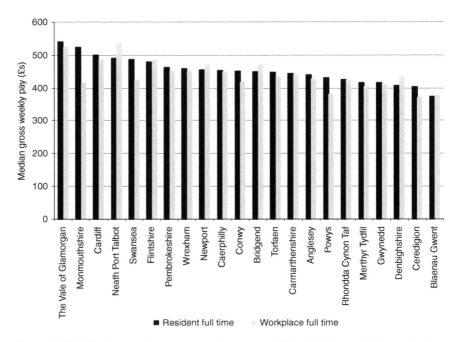

Figure 3.11 Full-time median gross weekly wages (£s) for both those living and those employed within each unitary authority

Source: Annual Survey of Hours and Earnings, 2010.

the Welsh average, as do those within the south east Wales valleys, with workers living in Blaenau Gwent having the lowest average full-time wage in Wales at £373.80 per week. Earnings tend to reflect the occupation structure discussed earlier (see section on Occupation, above). Authorities with larger proportions of the workforce employed as managers, directors and senior officials and professional occupations, such as those falling along the M4 corridor, had higher wage earners. Rural authorities, such as Monmouthshire, also follow this pattern, perhaps because of the large share of managers, directors and senior officials who lived there. Those areas with lower wages are the areas of the country where semi-skilled occupations and process, plant and machine occupations tended to dominate. However, in north east Wales this is not the case – there are relatively few managers, directors and senior officials and professional occupations, but wages of residents and employees living in Flintshire and Wrexham were still relatively high for Wales, possibly due to cross-border commuting (see Chapter 5). In a number of authorities, resident full-time workers earned more on average than workplace full-time workers. This includes areas such as Monmouthshire, Swansea, Conwy, Powys and Ceredigion and may be indicative of out-commuting in these areas. The effect of wages is discussed in more detail in relation to the Central and West Coast Locality in Chapter 6.

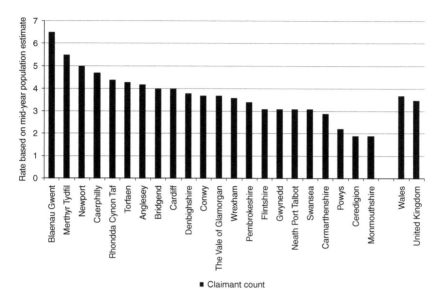

■ Claimant count

Figure 3.12 Percentage of people claiming Job Seeker's Allowance (JSA) and National Insurance credits by unitary authority

Source: DWP Claimant Count, 2010.

Claimant count

Figure 3.12 shows the claimant count rate by Welsh unitary authority for 2010. The Welsh rate of 3.7 per cent is slightly higher compared to the average for the UK at 3.5 per cent. The authorities in the south east Wales valleys make up five of the top six claimant count areas in Wales, with Blaenau Gwent having the highest proportion, with 6.5 per cent of the population claiming Jobseeker's Allowance (JSA) and National Insurance credits. Anglesey has the highest claimant count rate of the north Wales authorities. Rural authorities, such as Ceredigion, Monmouthshire, Powys and Carmarthenshire, have the lowest proportions of claim counts, with Ceredigion and Monmouthshire having only 1.9 per cent of the population claiming the benefits. There is a relationship between wages, occupation structure and qualifications such that areas with high claimant count rates tend to have lower weekly wages and a larger share of the population with no qualifications. However, this relationship is not so clear in authorities such as Cardiff, the Vale of Glamorgan, Conwy and Denbighshire, which have relatively high claimant count rates for Wales in comparison to the weekly wage rates. A more detailed discussion of aspects of the geography claimant count in Wales can be found in Chapter 6 in relation to the Central and West Coast Locality.

Mobility, accessibility and access to services

Mobility and accessibility in relation to commuting, methods of travelling to work and migration within and out of Wales varies across the country and is

interrelated with other socio-economic and cultural issues discussed in this chapter such as rates of economic activity, occupational profile, wage rates, Welsh
identity and Welsh-language use. Far more people commute out of, rather than
into, the south Wales valleys for work, for instance, while few people commute
out of their home authority in rural areas. The rates of migration into the valleys
from elsewhere are very low but much higher for rural areas, and particularly
migration from outside of Wales. Access to public services is also related to
mobility, with people living in rural areas having to travel a lot further to access
public services than those residing in urban areas. This section describes these
patterns and how they vary across Wales.

Commuting to work

According to the 2001 Census, well over 90 per cent of people in Wales who
commute to work do so to somewhere else in Wales. Only 3 per cent of people
commute to Wales from England, and 5.4 per cent of people commute to England
out of Wales. Very few people commute to and from Wales to other UK destinations.
As expected, most commuting between England and Wales occurs in authorities on
the Welsh border, with Flintshire, Wrexham, Monmouthshire, Powys, Denbighshire
and Conwy having the highest levels of cross-border commuting. More commuting
seems to take place between England and Wales in north and mid Wales than in
south Wales, perhaps reflecting transport routes and employment opportunities.

Figure 3.13 shows the percentage of all commuting in Wales which takes place
between Welsh unitary authorities. Generally, those commuting within Wales in

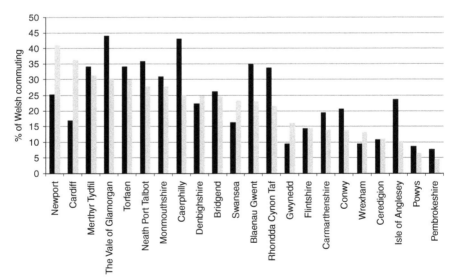

Figure 3.13 Percentage of people commuting between Welsh unitary authorities

Source: Census 2001.

rural areas, such as west Wales, work within the authority in which they live. This is particularly true of Pembrokeshire, Gwynedd and Powys, where less than 10 per cent of commuters move outside of their home authority. This is also true of those living in authorities containing large urban areas, such as Wrexham, Swansea and Cardiff, where only 10 per cent, 17 per cent and 16 per cent of commuters travel outside of their home authorities respectively. However, in south east Wales, there is more movement between authorities. Around 45 per cent of people living in the Vale of Glamorgan, who work in Wales, commute to another Welsh authority. This is also true for many of the south east Wales valley authorities, such as Caerphilly, where 43.1 per cent of people commute away from the authority. Authorities containing major cities, such as Newport, Cardiff, Wrexham and Swansea, have more people commuting into them than out of them, with 41 per cent, 36 per cent, 13 per cent and 23 per cent respectively. Over a third of people from the Vale of Glamorgan and the south east Wales valleys authorities commute out to find work in other unitary authorities, with few people commuting in. This reflects the lack of employment opportunities in the south east Wales valley authorities, and that a larger proportion of jobs, particularly lighter industry jobs, are based along the M4 corridor. Commuting is discussed in relation to employment in the Heads of the Valleys Locality and Welsh identity in the A55 Corridor Locality in chapters 4 and 5 respectively.

Mode of travel to work

According to the 2001 Census, just over two-thirds of people in Wales travel to work by private means, with only 6.5 per cent travelling by public transport, compared to over 14.8 per cent in England and 14.5 per cent in the rest of the UK (Figure 3.14). Cities such as Cardiff and Newport have the largest share of commuters travelling to work by public transport. Links can be drawn here to the areas where transport nodes are easier to access. Unsurprisingly, relatively few residents living in those areas without major transport links (rural areas in mid, west and the north west of the country) use public transport services. Communities accessible from south east Wales valley rail links, such as Merthyr Tydfil, Rhondda Cynon Taff and Caerphilly, also rate fairly high in terms of their residents' use of public transport. Travel to work is an important issue that is further discussed in relation to the Central and West Coast Locality in Chapter 6.

Migration

Milbourne (2011) discusses how migration has affected the population of Wales since the early 1980s, with a disproportional impact in rural Wales. He highlights three points concerning recent migration and demographic change in rural Wales that are discussed further in this and subsequent chapters: that population growth has resulted entirely from net in-migration; that population change has been uneven across different age groups; and those areas recording population losses and net out-movements of young people are also the areas where the Welsh language is strong. According to the 2001 Census over 80 per cent of migration

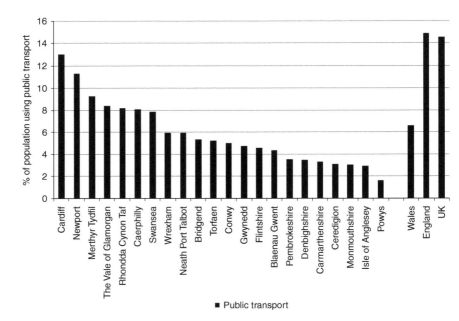

Figure 3.14 Percentage of the total population using public transport to travel to work by unitary authority

Source: Census 2001.

recorded in Wales between 2000 and 2001 is by people within Wales moving between Welsh authorities. Around 15 per cent of recorded migration is by people moving to England with less than 1 per cent moving to and from other parts of the UK. People moving into Wales accounted for 17 per cent of migration, so more people were moving into Wales than moving out in 2001. Figure 3.15 shows the migration taking place between Welsh unitary authorities and England. Authorities on the Welsh border in the east, such as Powys, Flintshire and Monmouthshire, have greater flows between the two countries than those in the west. However, areas in the north and west, such as Anglesey, Conwy, Gwynedd and Ceredigion, have large numbers of people migrating in from England, with relatively few people migrating out. These authorities contain popular retirement destinations and are well connected to England via the A55. This is also true of areas in the south west, such as Pembrokeshire and Carmarthenshire and the M4. Areas of south east Wales valleys, and Neath Port Talbot, have the lowest levels of migration to and from England. This may contribute to the large share of Welsh-born population and the strong feeling of Welsh national identity in these areas, with a high proportion of residents describing themselves as Welsh.

Of those moving within Wales, authorities along the M4 corridor seem to have the highest share of internal migration, with large numbers of people moving into and out of these areas (Figure 3.16). This is true of Monmouthshire, the Vale of

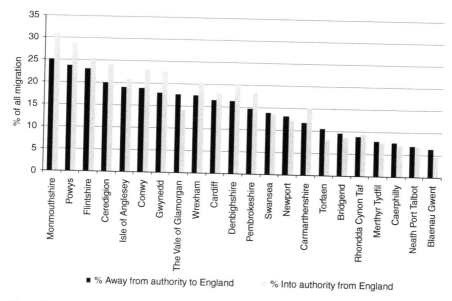

Figure 3.15 Percentage of people migrating between England and each Welsh unitary authority
Source: Census 2001.

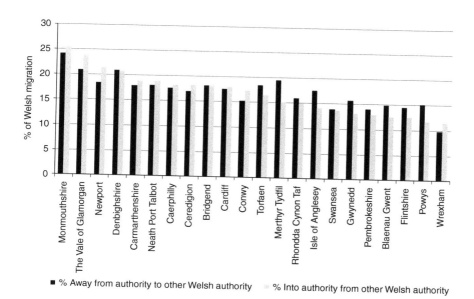

Figure 3.16 Percentage of migration occurring between each unitary authority
Source: Census 2001.

Glamorgan and Newport, where more people are moving in than out. Authorities within the south east Wales valleys, such as Torfaen, Merthyr Tydfil, Rhondda Cynon Taff and Blaenau Gwent, generally have more people moving out than moving in and migration tends to be between the different valley authorities than to elsewhere in Wales. Migration is a theme that is revisited in the three localities studies in chapters 4, 5 and 6.

Access to public services

Service provision in Wales is not just about the capacity of services to meet needs, but also involves issues relating to accessibility (Moles and Radcliffe, 2011). In Wales travel times to key services such as schools, GPs, food shops and post offices are, on average, less (by at least ten minutes) than travel times to other services, such as leisure centres and libraries (Table 3.5). However, travel times to dentists and secondary schools are longer on average. Average travel

Table 3.5 Average travel time in minutes to public services by unitary authority

	Average travel time (minutes)								
	To pri-mary school	To sec-ondary school	To NHS dentist	To GP sur-gery	To food shop	To post office	To li-brary	To leisure centre	To trans-port nodes
Blaenau Gwent	9	20	16	12	8	9	15	20	25
Bridgend	9	24	16	15	9	11	18	21	20
Caerphilly	9	20	16	12	8	10	17	20	17
Cardiff	8	20	11	9	7	10	15	16	20
Carmarthenshire	21	40	34	29	25	22	30	39	35
Ceredigion	30	51	57	46	36	33	54	52	57
Conwy	15	29	23	20	15	14	22	26	25
Denbighshire	16	28	24	19	15	16	25	28	37
Flintshire	11	23	20	15	12	13	19	23	22
Gwynedd	17	45	38	27	23	19	34	40	38
Isle of Anglesey	17	38	29	22	18	17	27	37	40
Merthyr Tydfil	9	23	17	13	8	9	20	18	20
Monmouthshire	22	35	27	26	20	23	32	36	35
Neath Port Talbot	9	21	19	14	9	10	16	21	24
Newport	9	23	14	12	8	10	17	24	22
Pembrokeshire	25	46	35	34	27	23	37	43	43
Powys	34	54	48	44	38	34	47	52	62
Rhondda Cynon Taf	8	24	18	12	8	9	16	24	18
Swansea	9	23	15	14	9	11	17	23	25
The Vale of Glamorgan	11	22	16	15	11	12	20	21	23
Torfaen	9	20	14	11	8	10	21	22	22
Wrexham	12	26	21	15	13	13	23	24	24

Source: Welsh Index of Multiple Deprivation, 2008.

times to transport nodes are also high, particularly in rural areas, and are reflected in statistics on the use of public transport across Wales.

Ceredigion has the lowest average travel time to different services and people living here have to travel around 30 minutes longer than people in Cardiff, who have the lowest average travel time across the range of services for Wales. With the exception of Monmouthshire, travel times to services in the north west and south west of Wales are longer than in other areas. This is particularly true in mid Wales authorities such as Powys and Ceredigion, where, on average, it takes at least ten minutes longer to travel to a service than in other parts of the west. Average travel times across the rest of Wales are fairly similar although, broadly speaking, it takes less time to get to a service in south east Wales and the south Wales valley areas, than it does in the north east of the country.

Access to internet broadband provision

Figure 3.17 clearly demonstrates that access to internet broadband provision varies greatly across Wales (Welsh Assembly Government, 2009). As is generally the case elsewhere in the UK, rural areas of Wales have greater numbers of broadband 'not spots' (locations where access to broadband is limited or non-existent) than the more densely-populated urban areas. This is particularly true of mid Wales authorities such as Ceredigion, Powys and Carmarthenshire, which, together, account for over half the total reported broadband 'not spots' in the country. Pembrokeshire, in the south west, and areas of north Wales, particularly

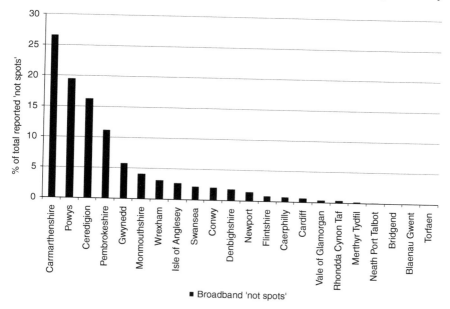

Figure 3.17 Percentage of total reported broadband 'not spots' by unitary authority

Source: Welsh Assembly Government, 2009.

Gwynedd and, maybe more surprisingly due to its status as one of the larger Welsh urban areas, Wrexham, also have high numbers of reported 'not spots'. In the south east of the country, with the exception of the rural authority of Monmouthshire, far fewer broadband 'not spots' have been reported, with the authorities of Neath Port Talbot, Merthyr Tydfil and Rhondda Cynon Taff having the fewest. The authority of Flintshire, in the north east, also has relatively few broadband 'not spots'. A more detailed analysis of broadband provision and 'not spots' relating to the Central and West Coast Locality can be found in Chapter 6.

Welsh identity, ethnicity and language

Wales has a distinct cultural identity which in some parts of the country is tied strongly to the use of the Welsh language. There are interesting relationships between a person's country of birth, their Welsh-language skills and their Welsh identity which vary across the country. There are also important links with mobility – the patterns of commuting and migration in an area – and also with the prevalence of second home ownership. This section describes these interlocking relationships and how they vary across Wales.

Welsh identity and ethnicity

Nearly two-thirds of people in Wales report themselves to be of Welsh nationality (Table 3.6). An even greater percentage of those who were born in Wales, report themselves to be Welsh, at just under 85 per cent. Despite the high numbers of people identifying as being Welsh, only 25 per cent of all people living in Wales are reported to speak Welsh (Annual Population Survey, 2010). Larger propor-tions of residents of south Wales identify as Welsh, with the highest proportions living in Rhondda Cynon Taff, Merthyr Tydfil, Blaenau Gwent, Caerphilly and Torfaen, followed closely by Neath Port Talbot and Bridgend. In contrast Gwynedd, Ceredigion and Swansea are close to the Welsh average, reflecting the make-up of the population in these areas. Those areas with the lowest number of people identifying as Welsh include Flintshire, Conwy and Denbighshire and other areas along the Welsh border, such as Powys, Wrexham and Monmouthshire. However, there is not a linear trend with distance from the border regarding the share of the population identifying as Welsh and other factors such as migration may play a role here (see Day, 2011, and Milbourne, 2011, for a more detailed discussion of the impact of migration on Welsh identity). These are explored in more detail in relation to the A55 corridor locality in Chapter 5.

The overwhelming majority of the Welsh population described their ethnicity as white (around 98 per cent) in the 2001 Census. People from ethnic back-grounds other than white were predominately Asian or mixed ethnic origin. Very few people described their ethnicity as black. People from non-white ethnic backgrounds in Wales were concentrated in Cardiff, Swansea and Newport, with almost 10 per cent of the population in Cardiff coming from a non-white ethnic background. People from non-white ethnic backgrounds also tended to be younger, with very few above the working age and almost half of the mixed ethnic population being under the age of 16.

Welsh language

Comparing aggregate figures on the proportions of people who speak Welsh with those who report their nationality as Welsh at the unitary authority level reveals an interesting paradox (Table 3.6). Bridgend Unitary Authority, for example, has one of the highest figures for the proportion of residents identifying themselves as Welsh but has the lowest proportion of Welsh speakers. Other areas of south Wales that have the highest proportion of those identifying as Welsh also have relatively small proportions of Welsh speakers. For instance, over 80 per cent of the population of Rhondda Cynon Taff regard themselves as Welsh, but only 18 per cent are able to speak the language. Areas in west and north Wales, including Gwynedd (71 per cent), Anglesey (62 per cent), Ceredigion (54 per cent) and Carmarthenshire (48 per cent) make up the top four Welsh-speaking unitary

Table 3.6 National identities and Welsh-language ability by unitary authority

	% British	% English	% Welsh	% Welsh-born national identity Welsh	% speak Welsh
Blaenau Gwent	24.1	4.4	82.1	88.7	16.2
Bridgend	33.1	6.4	73.4	85.5	16.0
Caerphilly	23.4	5.2	76.8	86.1	19.3
Cardiff	39.2	6.5	60.3	79.9	18.6
Carmarthenshire	18.3	10.3	72.9	92.5	47.5
Ceredigion	29.3	18.3	54.9	87.0	53.9
Conwy	42.2	15.2	46.1	79.9	34.1
Denbighshire	37.7	17.8	48.6	79.2	31.1
Flintshire	43.0	18.5	43.0	78.1	26.3
Gwynedd	29.6	10.9	63.9	89.3	71.8
Isle of Anglesey	33.7	12.7	58.0	85.8	62.2
Merthyr Tydfil	23.6	3.8	82.2	89.7	18.4
Monmouthshire	42.7	14.9	52.6	80.5	17.2
Neath Port Talbot	28.8	4.2	75.1	84.9	19.3
Newport	31.6	7.2	65.2	81.0	19.5
Pembrokeshire	24.4	13.6	62.4	87.4	16.9
Powys	34.9	18.3	50.8	83.9	24.4
Rhondda Cynon Taf	23.6	3.4	82.7	90.6	18.7
Swansea	30.1	4.9	66.9	81.5	16.7
The Vale of Glamorgan	35.5	7.9	66.5	83.3	17.5
Torfaen	26.8	5.7	75.3	85.8	18.8
Wrexham	30.9	12.3	59.5	83.5	17.6
Wales	31.3	9.3	65.0	84.8	25.6
England	43.1	56.1	0.7	–	–

Source: Annual Population Survey, 2010.

authorities. In contrast, there are fewer speakers in north east Wales, with Wrexham, as with other areas on the English border, having a lower percentage than the Wales average. Issues of Welsh-language use are revisited with regard to the A55 corridor locality in Chapter 5 and the Central and West Coast Locality in Chapter 6 and in detail in Jones (2012) and Milbourne (2011).

Second residences and holiday homes

The growth of second residences and holiday homes in Wales is a contentious political, social and cultural issue in Wales, as in other parts of the UK. The growth of second homes is regarded as one of the principal drivers of house prices in some parts of rural Wales leading to claims that local people are being priced out of the market for private accommodation (Milbourne, 2011). This is seen as a real issue in Welsh-speaking rural communities, with the owners of the second homes tending not to be Welsh speakers. There is also the fear that as second home ownership increases in some communities, local services and amenities will suffer due to the fall in potential demand stemming from fewer numbers of permanent residents. Census 2001 data reported (see Table 3.7) that, of all the household spaces within Wales, 1.2 per cent are second residences or holiday homes. This is nearly double the proportions seen in England (0.64 per cent) and the UK (0.73 per cent). Table 3.7 illustrates where second home ownership is potentially a problem. Far higher proportions of dwellings are holiday homes in the sparsely populated areas of mid and west Wales, particularly along the coastline country. There are proportionally far fewer second homes in south Wales and north east Wales, although there are exceptions such as the Gower peninsula, the Vale of Glamorgan and Cardiff Bay.

Deprivation and neighbourhood attitudes: the classification of small areas

Previous sections have drawn on secondary data sources at a range of aggregate scales to provide an overview of the demographic, socio-economic and cultural geography of Wales. However, areas within Wales have also been classified at more detailed spatial scales through a combination of variables drawn from sources such as the Census. This section will discuss two such classifications. The first is the commonly used WIMD, a classification of small area deprivation using a variety of variables, some of which have been discussed previously. The second is a classification developed by WISERD and is based on people's attitudes to their neighbourhood constructed from data in the annual Living in Wales survey. Both classifications show strong spatial patterning that can be related to the demographic, economic and cultural characteristics of Wales.

Welsh Index of Multiple Deprivation (WIMD) 2011

The WIMD 2011 can be used to describe patterns of social deprivation across Wales at Lower LSOA level based on a number of 'domains': income,

Table 3.7 Percentage of household spaces reported as being second residences and holiday homes by unitary authority

	Percentage second residences or holiday homes
Gwynedd	7.8
Pembrokeshire	6.1
Isle of Anglesey	3.7
Ceredigion	2.9
Conwy	2.2
Powys	2.2
Denbighshire	0.8
Monmouthshire	0.8
Swansea	0.7
Carmarthenshire	0.7
The Vale of Glamorgan	0.4
Bridgend	0.3
Wrexham	0.2
Cardiff	0.2
Flintshire	0.2
Merthyr Tydfil	0.2
Neath Port Talbot	0.2
Rhondda Cynon Taf	0.2
Newport	0.2
Blaenau Gwent	0.1
Caerphilly	0.1
Torfaen	0.1
Wales	1.2
England	0.6
UK	0.7

Source: Census 2001.

employment, health, education, access to services, housing, physical environment and community safety (Welsh Government, 2011). Each criterion is assessed and scored individually and each LSOA assigned a rank based on the score. An overall weighted score is also created based on the score of each criterion. LSOAs are also ranked by the overall score. The higher the score the more deprived the area. Figure 3.18 shows that the areas with the highest scores are situated in the south Wales valleys and along the coast of north Wales. A large area of Wales, particularly the rural areas such as mid and west Wales, has relatively low levels of deprivation on this measure, although pockets of deprivation still exist here. Some of the widest disparities in terms of WIMD scores at the LSOA level appear in Cardiff, Swansea and Wrexham.

WISERD's Wales neighbourhood typology

The Living in Wales survey asks eight attitudinal questions each year on aspects of local neighbourhood and the people who live there. Responses for these eight questions were pooled at MSOA level for each year from 2004–7,

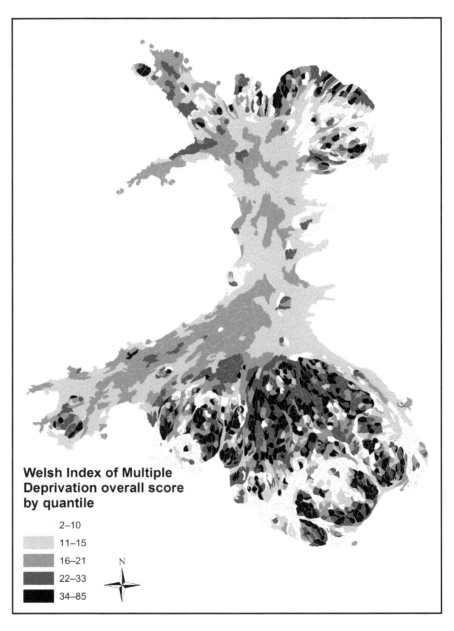

Welsh Index of Multiple
Deprivation overall score
by quantile

2–10
11–15
16–21
22–33
34–85

N

Figure 3.18 Overall scores of Welsh Index of Multiple Deprivation 2011 by LSOA

Source: Welsh Index of Multiple Deprivation, 2011.
Contains National Statistics data © Crown copyright and database right 2012.
Contains Ordnance Survey data © Crown copyright and database right 2012.

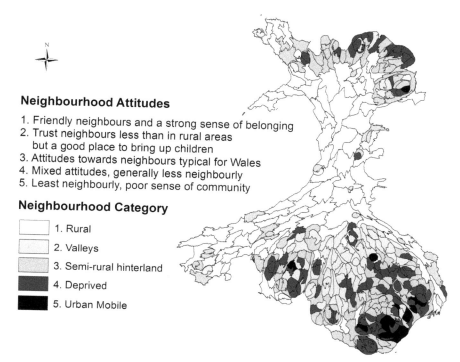

Neighbourhood Attitudes

1. Friendly neighbours and a strong sense of belonging
2. Trust neighbours less than in rural areas but a good place to bring up children
3. Attitudes towards neighbours typical for Wales
4. Mixed attitudes, generally less neighbourly
5. Least neighbourly, poor sense of community

Neighbourhood Category

1. Rural
2. Valleys
3. Semi-rural hinterland
4. Deprived
5. Urban Mobile

Figure 3.19 A classification of MSOAs using Welsh social attitudes data

Source: Living in Wales, 2004–7.
Contains National Statistics data © Crown copyright and database right 2012.
Contains Ordnance Survey data © Crown copyright and database right 2012.

and entered into a cluster analysis. This analysis divided the MSOAs into five neighbourhood types, reflecting the attitudes of the residents, and is shown in Figure 3.19. Neighbourhood 1 (608,100 people, 15,552 km^2) areas are predominately rural and characterised by people who trust most of their neighbours and who believe that their neighbourhood is a very good place to bring up children. Over half talk to their neighbours on most days, and regard their friendship as meaning a lot to them. They tend to ask their neighbours for advice and for favours and to borrow things from them. They have a very good sense of belonging to the area, tend to see themselves as similar to other people in their area and are willing to work with others to improve the neighbourhood. These neighbourhoods are predominately rural and are concentrated in mid, west and north west Wales.

Neighbourhood 2 (566,500 people, 1,223 km^2) areas are almost exclusively found, and almost entirely compose, the neighbourhoods of the Welsh valleys. These are former coal-mining communities that have experienced deindustrialisation and population loss since the mid-twentieth century (for more discussion, see Chapter 4). The only other areas outside of the valleys where these neighbourhoods can be found are in the former slate-mining communities of north west Wales and a few neighbourhoods in north east Wales. This neighbourhood is characterised by people whose attitudes are quite similar to those in neighbourhood type 1, with two main exceptions. The first is that they trust their neighbours a lot less than in neighbourhood type 1, with less than half trusting most of their neighbours and a quarter trusting very few of them. The second is that only a quarter believe that their neighbourhood is a very good place to bring up children, although half think that it is a fairly good place.

Neighbourhood 3 (952,300 people, 2,942 km^2) areas are predominately found in the suburbs of the cities in south Wales or the semi-rural hinterlands that surround them. They can also be found in the more affluent areas of the coastal fringe of north Wales and the market towns of mid Wales. The attitudes to neighbours and neighbourhood tend to reflect that of the Welsh average. Neighbourhood 4 (656,500 people, 627 km^2) areas are located in more deprived areas of Wales and generally outside of the former mining communities. They are concentrated in the south Wales urban areas and the coastal fringe of north Wales. They are characterised by people with a mix of attitudes towards their neighbourhood. Compared with the previous neighbourhood types, fewer people tended to agree strongly that they rely on their neighbours for advice, favours and friendship and fewer people strongly agreed that they have a sense of belonging to their neighbourhood and that they thought themselves as similar to their neighbours. Fewer people trust most of their neighbours, with a third trusting very few people at all. Despite this, around half believe that it's a fairly good place to bring up children, with a further fifth believing that it is a very good place.

Neighbourhood 5 (119,600 people, 37 km^2) areas are predominately found in the inner cities of Cardiff, Newport and Swansea and very rarely outside of these areas. They are not necessarily deprived areas (although some are), with this neighbourhood type including regenerated docklands. Instead, they are characterised by private rented accommodation and a very varied and mobile population. It is the smallest neighbourhood type and is perhaps the least neighbourly. Only a quarter trust many people in their neighbourhood and over half trust few people or no one at all. Two-fifths believe that it is a fairly good place to bring up children, but nearly one third think that it is a poor place. Fewer people talk to their neighbours compared to the other neighbourhood types, with a quarter talking to them less than once or month or never. Here, people are less likely than in the other neighbourhood types to see neighbours as friends and less likely to ask advice and favours from them. They have less of a sense of belonging and are less likely to see themselves as similar to others in their neighbourhood.

The patterning of the five neighbourhoods suggests that the attitudes of people in Wales towards the neighbourhood in which they live are broadly very similar – people living in similar places broadly share similar attitudes. Moreover, the analysis suggests that these attitudes are strongly embedded within particular parts of Wales, allowing this interesting geography to emerge. The distinctive clustering of neighbourhood 2 within the Welsh valleys, but rarely outside of this area, is a good example of this strong spatial clustering in attitudes. The distinctive rural neighbourhood type 1 is another example. They also broadly conform to other metrics used to classify Wales at small scales, such as deprivation indicators, commuting patterns and local labour market areas. This association suggests that people's attitudes towards their neighbours and their neighbourhood are broadly related to socio-economic, demographic and cultural factors that vary across Wales.

Conclusions

By mapping, graphing and describing the geographic distribution of the Welsh population across a variety of themes relating to demography, labour markets, workforce, identity and mobility, this chapter has demonstrated the diversity of the country with respect to socio-economic and cultural characteristics. Many of the variables show strong spatial patterning such as the strong levels of deprivation in the Welsh valleys, the importance of transport corridors in relation to the workforce, occupation and skills, the differences in the relationship between Welsh identity, Welsh-language use and country of birth in the north and south of the country, and the tensions brought about by migration and second homes. Moreover, similar spatial patterns appear to arise regardless of the variable being investigated, suggesting that Wales can be broadly divided into distinct regions: Cardiff and the M4 corridor; the Welsh valleys; central and the west coast; the north west Wales heartland; and the affluent rural and deprived coast of north east Wales. Each of these regions has distinct socio-economic spatial patterns and they also broadly conform to the Wales Spatial Plan areas. Researchers within WISERD have selected parts of four of these regions to investigate these types of issues in more detail: the Heads of the Valleys, the central and west coast and the A55 corridor (taking in the north west Wales heartland and the affluent rural and deprived coast of north east Wales). These are discussed in chapters 4, 5 and 6 with reference to the types of salient socio-economic and cultural issues characteristic of each locality.

References

Day, G. (2011) 'The Englishing of rural Wales? Migration, conflict and integration in community life', in Milbourne, P. (ed.), *Rural Wales in the Twenty-First Century: Society, Economy and Environment*. Cardiff: University of Wales Press.

Fevre, R., (1999) 'The Welsh Economy', in Dunkerley, D. and Thompson, A. (eds), *Wales Today*. Cardiff: University of Wales Press.

Herbert, D. T. (1980) 'Urban deprivation and urban policy', in Rees, G. and Rees, T. L. (eds), *Poverty and Social Inequality in Wales*. London: Croom Helm.

Higgs, G. and White, S. D. (1998) 'A comparison of community level indices in measuring disadvantage in Wales', in Day, G. and Thomas, D. (eds), *Contemporary Wales*, 10, 127–70.

Jones, H. (2012) *A Statistical Overview of the Welsh Language*. Cardiff: Welsh Language Board.

Milbourne, P. (2011) 'The social and cultural impacts of English migration to rural Wales', in Milbourne, P. (ed.), *Rural Wales in the Twenty-First Century: Society, Economy and Environment*. Cardiff: University of Wales Press.

Moles, K. and Radcliffe, J. (2011) 'Deep rural communities: exploring service provision in rural Wales', in Milbourne, P. (ed.), *Rural Wales in the Twenty-First Century: Society, Economy and Environment*. Cardiff: University of Wales Press.

Office for National Statistics (2012) 2011 Census: Population and Household Estimates for Wales, March 2011, *Statistical Bulletin*. Available at: http://www.ons.gov.uk/ons/ dcp171778_272571.pdf. Accessed: 22 April 2015.

Senior, M. (1998) 'Area variations in self-perceived limiting long term illness in Britain, 1991: is the Welsh experience exceptional?', *Regional Studies*, 32(3), 265–80.

Welsh Assembly Government (2009) Details of self-registrations made to the Broadband Notspot Registrations Website. Available at: http://gov.wales/docs/det/publications/ 090820broadbandnotspotregs.pdf. Accessed: 22 April 2015.

Welsh Government (2011) *Welsh Index of Multiple Deprivation 2011: Technical Report*. Cardiff: Welsh Government.

Woods, M. (2011) 'Market towns in rural Wales: a differentiated geography', in Milbourne, P. (ed.), *Rural Wales in the Twenty-First Century: Society, Economy and Environment*. Cardiff: University of Wales Press.

4   The Heads of the Valleys

Stephen Burgess and Kate Moles

Introduction

Few places could better illustrate the complexities of locality making than the Heads of the Valleys. The area selected as the south Wales WISERD locality is today highly recognisable as a locality of both political and popular construction. It is enshrined in much Welsh government policy and recognised as a particular bounded space by many stakeholders working in the area. The Heads of the Valleys is also recognisable as an area characterised politically as suffering specific, acute and long-standing social and economic challenges as the result of economic restructuring throughout the twentieth century. For this reason, it can be thought of as a problematic locality. However, this political construction has not always been so. The south Wales valleys were not always framed as suffering from socio-economic hardship, and the Heads of the Valleys was not always invoked as a political area.

This chapter traces the historical journey through which the Heads of the Valleys has come to be constructed as a locality, and characterised as an area with particular socio-economic challenges including low educational attainment, a low skill base and high levels of unemployment and economic inactivity. This is done through WISERD Knowing Localities Stakeholder Interviews.

The south Wales valleys: a history

The history of the Heads of the Valleys as a problematic political locality extends back nearly 100 years. At the centre of this story is a well-rehearsed history of industrial decline in the south Wales valleys that is important for understanding the Heads of the Valleys as it appears in policy today (David and Blewitt, 2004). It is important because of the two ways that this history may be thought of as 'worn'. Firstly, the story of industrial and economic decline is well worn in the sense that it has longevity: as we shall illustrate, declining economic fortunes of the south Wales valleys have provided their context for decades. Secondly, this history of the valleys is also well worn in the sense that post-industrial decline is a narrative and characterisation that has been borne by the area. The past is a resource that is drawn upon in the construction of place identities to sustain the idea of a coherent, cohesive population bound together historically and in social and cultural ways. These resources and identities may be exploited by various actors. For example, local residents' groups may use them to draw communities together and policy addressing south Wales has used them to characterise the area and frame the needs of the local population, providing part of the justification for strategic responses.

David Gilbert has argued that too often 'the complicated histories of mining communities have been ignored in imaginings which choose to read their distinctivenesses as evidence of isolation, homogeneity, apartness and sometimes of pathology or virtue' adding that '[w]e appear to be coming to the end of the history of the ways of life associated with coal-mining in Britain. It would add to the injustices of that ending if the lives of mining people were only remembered through one-dimensional evocations of the lost world of the mining community' (Gilbert, 1995: 53). However, there is, arguably, a tendency towards this in the south Wales valleys, where the well-rehearsed history of industrial decline and consequent post-industrial characterisation of the area within policy simultaneously align them with the particular maladies they are seeking to address. This process leads to the production of a problematic and persistent narrative in which both the area and its residents are characterised in particular ways. The same picture of the valleys is continually represented, and so the characterisation of the area is sustained and cyclical in nature.

The Heads of the Valleys: different spatial framing, 'same old problem'

The creation of the Heads of the Valleys as a post-industrial region with particular needs can be traced back to the 1920s and 1930s. As a consequence of historic socio-economic trends, including the restructuring of the UK economy, basic industries at this time (coal, iron and steel, shipbuilding, heavy engineering and textiles) declined, resulting in severe localised unemployment and impacting on living conditions in areas previously economically dependent upon these industries (Page, 1976). The area now known as the Heads of the Valleys suffered keenly from this process.

At first these areas were characterised as 'derelict' or 'depressed' and the recession following the First World War, alongside changing patterns of coal consumption, drew the south Wales coalfields into this category (David and Blewitt, 2004). The UK government responded by passing three enactments between 1934 and 1937, collectively known as the Special Areas legislation, whose influence was felt in the long term and which have been described as a landmark in UK economic policy (Page, 1976). In doing so, the nomenclature of these emerging areas of economic hardship was made less negative. The first of these, the Special Areas (Development and Improvement) Act of 1934, provided for the appointment of two commissioners (one for England and Wales and another for Scotland) charged with working across various government and civil society actors to develop and improve areas affected by industrial depression, with a particular focus on providing employment (The National Archives, 2013). The Special Areas identified included 'most of south Wales' (ibid.). The remaining two Acts (1936, 1937) variously furthered the aims of the 1934 Act (ibid.; Page, 1976). This, arguably, was the beginning of the political perception of south Wales as a problematic region characterised by post-industrial depression. As we shall see, over time this designation of 'south Wales' or the 'south Wales valleys' became more nuanced, and out of this nuance emerged the Heads of the Valleys as a sub-region within Welsh policy.

Over the next 30 years or so, while reference to regional socio-economic challenges was mostly made to the south Wales valleys in general, or individual valleys and towns in particular, a sub-regional geography emerged. A search of Historic Hansard Online revealed that during the late 1950s and early 1960s there were a series of references in Westminster to the development of the Heads of the Valleys road. Reflecting local feeling regarding the necessity of transport infrastructure to tackle the challenges of the area, it appears as though the Heads of the Valleys began to be framed as a particular post-industrial area, with particular challenges, requiring a specific policy focus. For example, in the House of Lords in 1959, Lord Granville-west stated that given already poor road connections, possible cuts to rail services serving the Heads of the Valleys would confound the attraction of new industry to a post-industrial area (House of Lords Hansard Parliamentary Debates, 1959). Here, post-industrial challenges facing the Heads of the Valleys were framed as a consequence of their geography and the notion of a sub-regional geography was emerging among politicians.

This sub-regional geography of south Wales, including an emerging Heads of the Valleys, was further embedded in policy in 1967, with the publication of *Wales: The Way Ahead*, written by the then recently established Welsh Office (David and Blewitt, 2004; Osmond, 2008) and building on previous regional policies in Wales such as *Depopulation in mid-Wales* (Hughes and Mordey, 1974) and the *Buchannan Report* (Coop and Thomas, 2007). Some have argued that this was a turning point in the direction of planning strategy for Wales (Hughes and Mordey, 1974).

The document was in effect an audit of the current state of Wales, divided into four sections: resources; material prosperity; the environment; and problems of particular areas. Five particular 'areas' of Wales were identified, each being characterised as having different resource, material prosperity and environmental problems. One of these areas was 'Industrial south Wales', defined as 'extending some 80 miles along the coast roughly from Kidwelly in the west to Chepstow in the east and up to 30 miles in depth' (Welsh Office, 1967: 101).

Industrial south Wales was further divided into regions with differently perceived needs and potentialities. On one hand, the valley mouths, nearer the coastal belt, were seen as favourable for development and growth. In contrast, the rest of the valleys described as 'mountainous country deeply dissected by valleys, many of which are narrow' (ibid., 101) were seen as posing a greater challenge to development. Reflecting debate in central government (see above), *Wales: The Way Ahead* placed considerable importance on the recent completion and future extension of the Heads of the Valleys road to serve and encourage growth in the non-coastal plain areas of the south Wales valleys. Although the term 'Heads of the Valleys' was not used to define the area itself, a sub-regional geography of a problematic Heads of the Valleys, as a geographical contrast to the less problematic, better connected and flatter areas nearer the city cores of Newport, Cardiff and Swansea can again be seen emerging.

The Heads of the Valleys road continued to have a role in creating this political locality, being seen as necessary to assure the growth of upper valleys towns such as Merthyr Tydfil, Aberdare, Tregedar and Brynmawr, and also serving as a metaphor for challenges such as accessibility and geographical location which were seen to hinder the post-industrial growth of these upper valleys areas. The document characterised what was seen as the uniquely problematic upper valleys as an area facing unemployment as a consequence of the economic restructuring outlined above, but at the same time as an area where it was impossible to meet all employment needs locally. Thus the importance of an integrated development plan for south Wales, including socio-economic connections between the upper valleys and the valley mouths and the major cities of the coastal plain, was flagged.

Thirteen years later, and a politically constructed locality called the Heads of the Valleys was being discussed in Westminster during a debate in December 1979, with reference to the ongoing socio-economic challenges facing the area (House of Commons Hansard Parliamentary Debates, 1979). This reflected changes at the local level, where the Heads of the Valleys was becoming a recognised political locality. For example, following *the Wales: The Way Ahead* agenda, plans for the development of a new town at the valley mouth town of Llantrisant, with the aim of attracting migration from the Rhondda Valley for employment and housing, were abandoned under pressure from the Heads of the Valleys authorities, who saw it as a threat to their long-term survival (David and Blewitt, 2004). The Heads of the Valleys was gaining capital as a politically constructed locality. At the national level, there is little evidence of a Welsh planning agenda until 1988 and what does exist favours regional development, as is reflected in the development of policies such as the Valleys Programme in 1988 (Tewdwr-Jones, 2002).

Arguably, the next political landmark in the creation of the Heads of the Valleys locality was Welsh devolution in 1999. Following devolution in Wales, the construction of the Heads of the Valleys that had developed across the latter half of the twentieth century, characterised by a lack of socio-economic development since the restructuring of the economic base, became entrenched in Welsh policy. Policies were developed to try and halt the perceived cycles of poverty and deprivation that trapped and defined the area. The 2000 Welsh Index of Multiple Deprivation highlighted significant inequality in Wales, with high poverty in the south Wales valleys (Adamson, 2010). In response, the Welsh government has concentrated on area-based regeneration policy to address such inequality, making a special case for the Heads of the Valleys within these policies. Since 1999, the Welsh government has delineated the Heads of the Valleys as a policy area in order that policy may be focused upon it.

The Heads of the Valleys region, as it is currently defined, is situated at the northern edge of the area known as the south Wales valleys, bordered by the A465 Heads of the Valleys road. The boundary includes all of Merthyr Tydfil and Blaenau Gwent local authorities, and parts of Rhondda Cynon Taf, Caerphilly and Torfaen (see Figure 4.1).

Throughout the post-devolution period, there have been a series of policies which have evidenced the construction of the Heads of the Valleys as a particular and problematic locality. Firstly, there are policies which highlight the particular needs of the south Wales valleys. For example, the 2002 national economic strategy *A Winning Wales* highlighted the south Wales valleys as 'lagging behind on most measures' (Welsh Assembly Government, 2002: 106). Also, since devolution, the area 'west Wales and the Valleys', which includes the Heads of the Valleys authorities (WEFO, 2013), has been eligible for European Structural and Cohesion Funding, aimed at reducing economic inequality across the European region (Objective 1 funding between 2000 and 2006 and Convergence Funding between 2007 and 2013) (Boland, 2004; European Commission, 2011a, b). Secondly, other policies, such as the 2007 coalition agreement *One Wales*, adopt the Heads of the Valleys region in particular.

The Wales Spatial Plans (Welsh Assembly Government, 2004, 2008) were key in further defining the Heads of the Valleys as a politically envisaged locality. The positioning of the Heads of the Valleys in the Wales Spatial Plan (WSP) marked a significant formalising of its position within south Wales political and policy discourses. In the first WSP (2004), the Heads of the Valleys was identified as a particular sub-area of the south east Wales region. The Heads of the Valleys was clearly framed as a problematic political locality, the characterisation of which rehearsed long-standing discourses of the south Wales valleys as an area of homogeneous socio-economic challenges. The plan stated that the south Wales valleys 'have a high concentration of social deprivation and economic inactivity, allied to low levels of educational attainment and skills, poor *health and a declining population*' Welsh Assembly Government, 2004: 49, emphasis added). Echoing *Wales: The Way Ahead*, the south east Wales region was constructed with the aim that the relative prosperity of Cardiff was to be shared in order to address the socio-economic disparities across south east Wales. Again, the Heads of the Valleys (or upper valleys) was seen as having more problems than other valleys locations:

> The valley communities have diverse characteristics and needs. This ranges from geographically isolated valley communities to many of the lower and middle valleys which are becoming increasingly buoyant in both economic and social terms.
>
> (Ibid.: 50)

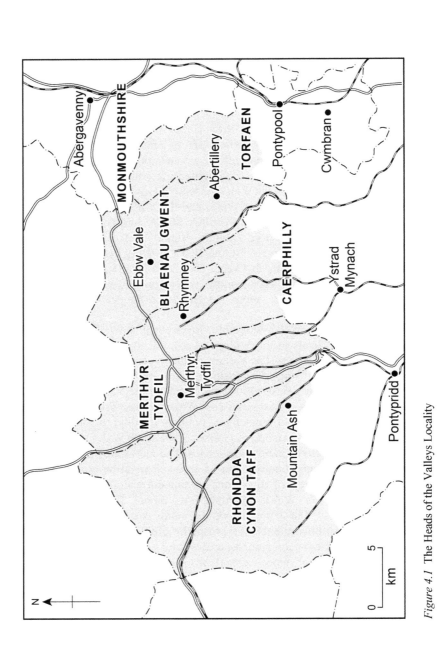

Figure 4.1 The Heads of the Valleys Locality

Source: Mastermap Layer@Crown Copyright/database right 2010.

Placing the reasoning for this on the proximity of the middle and lower valleys to the prosperous coastal belt, a strategy for the relatively worse-off Heads of the Valleys was outlined. This was to be achieved by a focus on increased infrastructure and connectivity, with a principal focus on improving transport in order to create an integrated transport network. This strategy centred on the upgrading of the A465 Heads of the Valleys road alongside which would sit a 'joined-up' programme of regeneration along the Heads of the Valleys corridor to:

> improve quality of life, retain and attract residents, and increase the prosperity of the whole area focusing initially on the unlocking the [sic] potential of Merthyr Tydfil and Ebbw Vale.
>
> (Ibid.: 49)

The intention was that these centres would then act as catalysts for the regeneration of the upper valleys, which would involve a sustained increase in economic turnover, retail, housing and service provision, whilst retaining and attracting a socially mixed population across the Heads of the Valleys through improved linkages with surrounding neighbourhoods.

In the updated WSP (2008) the Heads of the Valleys area continued to be identified as a specific sub-division of the south east Wales region, the key difference being the expansion of the region further west, creating the Heads of the Valleys Plus area. The 2008 WSP characterises the Heads of the Valleys Plus as:

> An area set in superb natural surroundings, comprising the upper valleys of the Capital Region facing very considerable social challenges created by economic restructuring of the late 20th century.
>
> (Welsh Assembly Government, 2008: 99)

The story is presented straightforwardly; industrial decline has left a legacy of socio-economic inequality. Echoing the sentiment of the 2004 WSP, this is reinforced in the 2008 Wales Spatial Plan by the location of the Heads of the Valleys in the penumbra of Cardiff, the economic force of contemporary south east Wales. Physical, environmental and social regeneration are invoked in the 2008 WSP as having the potential to alter the internal and external perceptions of the Heads of the Valleys, allowing it to participate in the development of the Capital Region. Again, the symbolic lynch pin in this process was the upgrading (duelling) of the A465 Heads of the Valleys road, as it would increase the capacity for movement in and out of the area, and encourage the movement in of business and people.

Having identified the Heads of the Valleys as a specific area, with particular challenges, the now devolved Welsh government also created policy which specifically targeted this politically constructed locality. In 2005, as part of reactions to and implementation of the WSP, *'Heads – We Win ...' A Strategic Framework for the Heads of the Valleys* policy document established the Heads of the Valleys Programme (Welsh Assembly Government, 2005). Running until

2020, this programme would invest £140 million of Welsh government money in the Heads of the Valleys area. This document delivered a vision for the Heads of the Valleys which it suggested everyone could unite behind and which would only be achieved by 'working together and removing traditional barriers' (ibid.: 4):

> At the heart of this approach will be the proactive involvement of people in their own communities. Active, independent community groups are essential for building strong and inclusive communities within the Heads of the Valleys to provide support, services and opportunities.
>
> (Ibid.)

This vision was further embellished in June 2006, with the publication of *Turning Heads: A Strategy for the Heads of the Valleys 2020* (Welsh Assembly Government, 2006). This claimed widespread support for a Heads of the Valleys Programme following consultation around the *'Heads – We Win ...'* document, and set out a strategy for delivering the programme. The strategy explicitly (for example, see Welsh Assembly Government, 2005: 5) built on achievements of the programme to date. As such, it was taking forward the vision and understanding of the Heads of the Valleys outlined in *'Heads – We Win ...'*. The *Turning Heads* document says of itself that it:

> breathes life into a vibrant and new regeneration partnership between the public, private and voluntary/community sectors. Set firmly within the context of the Wales Spatial Plan, it sets out a shared vision for what the area will look and feel like by the year 2020 and the ways in which we will turn our vision into reality.
>
> (Welsh Assembly Government, 2006: 6)

Through these two policy documents, the Heads of the Valleys became reinforced as a problematic political locality characterised as facing socio-economic challenges as the result of economic restructuring over the first half of the twentieth century.

To summarise, the politicised definition of the Heads of the Valleys as a particular and problematic locality has been a long time in the making, leading to the creation of long-standing popular and political characterisations of the area. Many of the commonly cited characteristics of the south Wales valleys today are those which the 1934 Act set out to address: economic inactivity and unemployment, high levels of morbidity, under-developed communications, poor housing and low levels of workforce skills (Osmond, 2008). 'For seventy years, the south Wales Valleys have been eligible for just about every form of regional assistance that has been available' (Fothergill, 2008: 4). They are the oldest regeneration region in the UK, having been established as an area for economic assistance by the Special Areas Act in 1934 (Osmond, 2008).

Since devolution, the Heads of the Valleys has been more firmly entrenched in policy and has been classified as 'the most problematic part of the Valleys, furthest from the new investment in Cardiff and the M4 corridor' (Fothergill, 2008: 3). This has resulted in the concretisation of the Heads of the Valleys as a locality with particular issues, particular people and particular problems, which need further intervention.

The contemporary construction of the Heads of the Valleys has created a strong narrative and a clearly defined notion of locality. This reproduces and rehearses long-standing understandings about the place and its people which give it a particular theme in political discourse which, whilst it may be pertinent to the locality, does not always relate to wider trends. This has meant that, in general, policies targeted at achieving regeneration in the Heads of the Valleys have tended to focus on addressing issues related to the geography, infrastructure and population of the locality, often at the expense of locating and addressing these issues within broader structural, economic and social processes and patterns that are found throughout Wales, the UK and beyond. This has led to a narrative and political discourse which has tended to describe and classify the problems as being caused solely by these local factors rather than as part of a broader range of social and economic interactions.

This theme can also be traced through many of the regeneration initiatives implemented in the region. These too tend to focus on improvements to the area and its population often in isolation from consideration of broader global trends. This can be demonstrated through two key, and widely heralded, educational developments in the Heads of the Valleys: The Works in Ebbw Vale (Blaenau Gwent) and The College Merthyr Tydfil.

The Works, Ebbw Vale

There is perhaps no project more symbolic of the desire for socio-economic and material restructuring in the Heads of the Valleys than The Works in Ebbw Vale, Blaenau Gwent. The Works is a mixed-land use regeneration and redevelopment project for the former steelworks site, which describes itself as a 'new vision' for Ebbw Vale (The Works, 2013a) and promotes itself as the key to transforming the present and future of Ebbw Vale and, by example, both the rest of Blaenau Gwent and the wider Heads of the Valleys region (Blaenau Gwent County Borough Council, 2007; The Works, 2013a).

The development, ongoing since the closure of the (by then Corus) steelworks in July 2002, was seen to support objectives set out within *Turning Heads*, including those specific to Ebbw Vale, and to help address the need for changes to the economic structure of the area (Alan Baxter and Associates, 2010). The Masterplan, approved in July 2007, included the development of: land for employment use; a learning campus; a primary school; a new hospital; new homes; a railway terminus; a leisure centre; theatre; and offices (Blaenau Gwent County Borough Council, 2007; The Works, 2013b). At this time, the Minister for the Economy and Transport, Ieuan Wyn Jones, described The Works as an exemplar project 'designed to revitalise and regenerate this area of the Heads of the Valleys and ... a catalyst for change, creating social and environmental

benefits as well as employment opportunities and new facilities for future generations' (Blaenau Gwent County Borough Council, 2007).

The Works development represents the Welsh government's regeneration
outlook, working towards producing a space that engenders hope for the future
through a wide range of academic and vocational courses that will enable people
to develop skills, gain qualifications and compete in the job market. Working in
partnership with Blaenau Gwent County Borough Council, Coleg Gwent and the
University of Wales, Newport this development describes the position it will
occupy as being able to react to the changing demands of the local economy in
order to provide local residents with improved employment opportunities (The
Works, 2007, 2013c).

This is characteristic of the 'improvement from within' approach adopted by
policy-makers seeking to tackle the issues inherent in the Heads of the Valleys
locality. The establishment of The Works is predicated on the idea that, if you
provide space, businesses will relocate; this does not take into account wider
national or global factors. In addition, the belief that improving the education
and skill-sets of the people will subsequently improve the place is a popularly
conceived political notion also invoked by policy-makers in this case. What is
problematic is that these two factors are interdependent and should not be
considered in isolation from wider global factors influencing economic
development.

The College, Merthyr Tydfil

West across the Heads of the Valleys from Blaenau Gwent lies another of the
Heads of the Valleys authorities, Merthyr Tydfil. The College Merthyr Tydfil
(The College) is a tertiary college developed as the result of the reorganisation of
county-wide post-16 education. Development occurred to address a skills short-
age and consequently improve the economic outlook of both the immediate
population and the Heads of the Valleys more widely. The College is the result
of the merger of the existing Merthyr Tydfil Further Education College with sixth
forms across the county (The College Merthyr Tydfil, 2013a). Initially called the
Merthyr Learning Quarter (MLQ), it was renamed The College after a public
competition to rename it failed to find an 'acceptable' name (Merthyr Learning
Quarter, 2011).

The College is ensconced in strong discourses regarding the importance of
education in transforming both the educational qualifications of young people
and, as a result, transforming the area. This is encapsulated in The College's
mission statement (The College Merthyr Tydfil, 2013b) and also in its current
strategic plan, 'Raising aspirations and maximising potential' (University of
Glamorgan, 2012). These intentions followed through into institutional policy,
when the doors opened in September 2013, with the 2013/14–2015/16 strategic
plan for The College stating that '[t]he college will make a major impact on the
economy of the Heads of the Valleys region by increasing the acquisition of basic
and higher level skills and qualifications for employment or higher education, and

so support the development of healthy and sustainable communities' (University of Glamorgan, 2012).

Again, there is some indication for the recognition of the need to understand the requirements of local employers in order to produce an employable workforce (The College Merthyr Tydfil, 2013b; University of Glamorgan, 2012), although it is not possible to find evidence of these links being developed. Indeed, the strategic plan identifies issues regarding the lack of major employers in the area, and that where employers can be identified the current weak economic climate means that partnership working may be a challenge (University of Glamorgan, 2012). Again this emphasis on local employers and regional developments lacks outward focus and ignores trends taking place beyond the immediate locality.

The Heads of the Valleys: a locality invoked and applied by stakeholders

To conclude this discussion on the creation of the Heads of the Valleys as a politically created and popularly recognised locality, this section presents data on the construction and classification of the Heads of the Valleys as a locality by stakeholders who work in the area. Through discussions of their work, pictures emerged of what they understood constituted the Heads of the Valleys in relation to their daily activities within their policy arena.

Figure 4.2 shows the spatial ellipses of the places discussed in the interviews by stakeholders in the eight policy themes. Each ellipse represents the spatial focus of the stakeholder interviews for each policy theme and demonstrates how this varies in size and orientation. All the ellipses are centred on the Heads of the Valleys region, but some encompass much wider areas stretching into west and mid Wales. The smallest ellipse belongs to stakeholders working in the education and young people policy theme and this is closest to the Heads of the Valleys Spatial Plan area. The other policy themes that have a close fit with the Heads of the Valleys as defined in Figures 4.2 and 4.3 are health, wellbeing and social care and crime, public space and policing, although even these take in significant parts of south Powys. Interestingly, given the small ellipse for education and young people, the largest ellipse is for stakeholders in the employment and training policy area covering much of south east and mid Wales. The spatial ellipse for economic development and generation, falls between the two and, like the employment and training ellipse, is much larger than the Heads of the Valleys as defined in the Spatial Plan. All ellipses stretch down to Cardiff, reflecting not just the importance of the city coastal zone in the policy remit of the Heads of the Valleys Spatial Plan area but also the importance of the Welsh government in devolved policy-making.

What Figure 4.2 implies is that the Heads of the Valleys area is central to the work of all stakeholders. However, the work of most stakeholders goes beyond the boundaries of the Heads of the Valleys, although the extent to which this occurs is highly dependent on the policy theme they are working within. As all

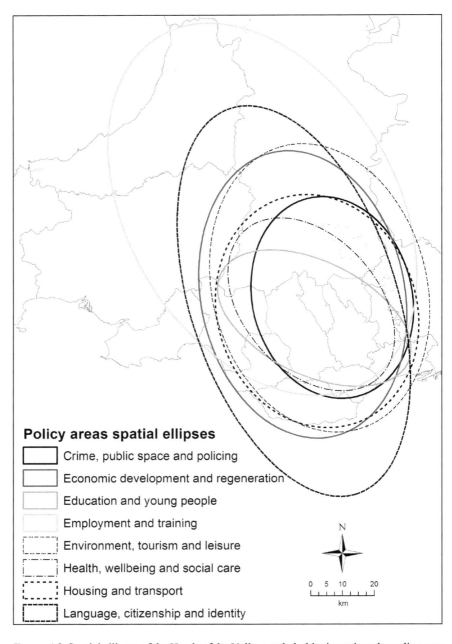

Policy areas spatial ellipses

- [ ] Crime, public space and policing
- [ ] Economic development and regeneration
- [ ] Education and young people
- [ ] Employment and training
- [ ] Environment, tourism and leisure
- [ ] Health, wellbeing and social care
- [ ] Housing and transport
- [ ] Language, citizenship and identity

N

0 5 10   20
km

Figure 4.2 Spatial ellipses of the Heads of the Valleys stakeholder interviews by policy area

Source: Heads of the Valleys stakeholder interviews.
Contains Ordnance Survey data © Crown copyright and database right 2012.

the spatial ellipses overlap, it is possible to extract an area that is common to all the stakeholders interviewed and define this as the core area that defines policy in the Heads of the Valleys. Such a process would allow the existing Heads of the Valleys boundary to be questioned and problematised in light of stakeholder practice. Figure 4.3 shows the core area in common for all eight policy themes and this is, indeed, centred on the Heads of the Valleys Plus area. An additional spatial ellipse is shown that has been derived from all the stakeholder interviews regardless of policy theme. This captures the core area but also illustrates the importance of south Powys and the areas immediately west of the Heads of the Valleys in the spatial focus of most stakeholders' activities.

Conclusions

The Heads of the Valleys is perceived in both popular and political discourse as a strong and commonly invoked contemporary locality with a history stretching back nearly 100 years. Over time, long-standing narratives of post-industrial decline have been appropriated in the south Wales valleys. The relevance of these narratives is clear: the Heads of the Valleys underperform, both in relation to the rest of Wales and the rest of the UK, across a series of economic and social measures – although the extent of this underperformance may be debated.

The decline of heavy industry in the Heads of the Valleys was the result of changing global patterns of production and consumption and illustrates the importance of the global economy in dictating local employment patterns. It is this global economy which politicians in the mid-1990s realised could no longer be attracted to south Wales. While policy turned to other strategies for economic regeneration, the importance of these global processes cannot be underestimated in mediating the extent to which simply increasing qualifications levels among the Heads of the Valleys population can lead to new business being attracted to the area. The location strategies of global multinational companies, for example, are based upon *global* geographies of factors such as infrastructure, costs (including wages), supply and demand. These are levers over which devolved Welsh policy can have no influence, but that must be recognised and taken into account when new policies which aim to regenerate the locality are created.

As noted above, the Heads of the Valleys has become a commonly invoked locality, recognised by many stakeholders. During the study, many formal and informal lines of enquiry with stakeholders working at Welsh government, local authority and equivalent levels, as to the origins of, and reasons for, the definition of the Heads of the Valleys, showed that they either did not know or were uncertain: there were many operating at relatively high levels of policy within the area, and who adopted the definition of the area as a locality, but did not know its purpose or background. However, they did understand the characterisation of the Heads of the Valleys as socio-economically poor, and that policy was targeting this. This suggests the strength of the politically constructed and reinforced locality within Wales: an acceptance of the Heads of the Valleys as a locality and a particular kind of area.

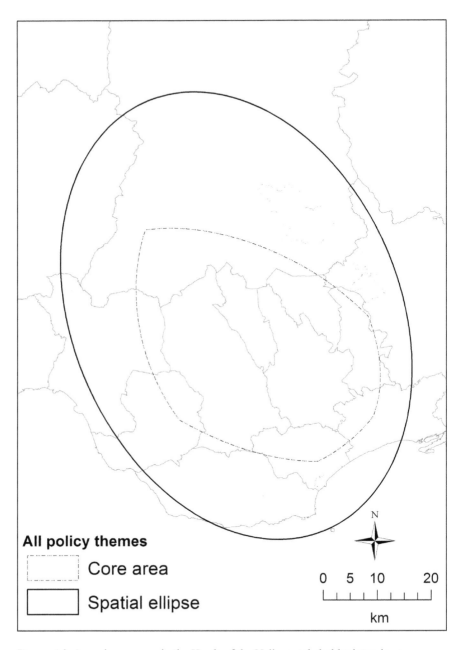

All policy themes

- - - - Core area

▢ Spatial ellipse

N

0   5   10   20

km

Figure 4.3 Areas in common in the Heads of the Valleys stakeholder interviews

Source: Heads of the Valleys stakeholder interviews.
Contains Ordnance Survey data © Crown copyright and database right 2012.

References

Adamson, D. (2010) 'Community empowerment. Identifying the barriers to "purposeful" citizen participation', *International Journal of Sociology and Social Policy*, 30(3/4), 114–26.

Alan Baxter and Associates (2010) *Former Steelworks Site, Ebbw Vale Outline Planning Application Masterplan Framework: Design & Access Statement*. London: Alan Baxter and Associates LLP. Available at: http://www.blaenau-gwent.gov.uk/documents/SD61a_Masterplan_Design_and_Access_Statement_The_Works_Update.pdf. Accessed: 17 February 2015.

Blaenau Gwent County Borough Council (2007) *Green Light For The Works: The £300 Million Project To Transform Former Ebbw Vale Steelworks Site*. Available at: http://www.blaenau-gwent.gov.uk/news/2007/9520.asp. Accessed: 16 July 2013.

Boland, P. (2004) 'Wales and Objective 1 Status: Learning the Lessons or Emulating the Errors?', *European Planning Studies*, 12(2), 249–70.

Coleg Gwent (2014) *Strategic Statements*. Available at: http://www.coleggwent.ac.uk/index.php?Pid=2381&Mid=2301. Accessed: 17 March 2014.

The College Merthyr Tydfil (2013a) *What is THE COLLEGE Merthyr Tydfil?* Available at: http://www.merthyr.ac.uk/content/your-college. Accessed: 19 July 2013.

The College Merthyr Tydfil (2013b) *Our Vision and Mission*. Available at http://www.merthyr.ac.uk/content/our-vision-and-mission. Accessed: 19 July 2013.

Coop, S. and Thomas, H. (2007) 'Planning doctrine as an element in planning history: the case of Cardiff', *Planning Perspectives*, 22, 167–93.

David, R. and Blewitt, N. (2004) *The Socio-Economic Characteristics of the South Wales Valleys in a Broader Context: A Report for the Welsh Assembly Government*. Cardiff: Institute of Welsh Affairs.

European Commission (2011a) *United Kingdom West Wales and the Valleys Objective 1 Programme*. Available at: http://ec.europa.eu/regional_policy/archive/country/prordn/details.cfm?gv_PAY=UK&gv_reg=ALL&gv_PGM=11&LAN=7&gv_PER=1&gv_defL=7. Accessed: 15 May 2013.

European Commission (2011b) *United Kingdom, Operational Programme 'West Wales and the Valleys': West Wales and the Valleys Programme under Convergence Objective, Co-funded by ERDF*. Available at: http://ec.europa.eu/regional_policy/archive/country/prordn/details_new.cfm?gv_PAY=UK&gv_reg=ALL&gv_PGM=1239&LAN=7&gv_PER=2&gv_defL=7. Accessed: 15 May 2013.

Fothergill, S. (2008) 'The most intractable development region in the UK', in Osmond, J. (ed.), *Futures for the Heads of the Valleys*. Cardiff: Institute of Welsh Affairs. 3–11.

Gilbert, D. (1995) 'Imagined communities and mining communities', *Labour History Review*, 60(2), 47–55.

House of Lords Hansard Parliamentary Debates (1959) 'British Transport Commission Debate', vol. 217, col. 246–8. Available at: http://hansard.millbanksystems.com/lords/1959/jun/25/british-transport-commission-bill#S5LV0217P0_19590625_HOL_12]. Accessed: 23 July 2013.

House of Commons Hansard Parliamentary Debates (1979) 'Heads of the Valleys Authorities Debate', vol. 847. Available at: http://hansard.millbanksystems.com/commons/1972/dec/06/heads-of-the-valleys-authorities. Accessed: 23 July 2013.

Hughes, T. E. V. and Mordey, R. A. (1974) 'Beyond "Wales: The Way Ahead"', *Cambria: A Welsh Geographical Review*, 1(1), 55–60.

Merthyr Learning Quarter (2011) *Merthyr Learning Quarter, Core Brief: Edition 4 – December 2011*. Available at: http://www.merthyr.gov.uk/english/councilanddemocracy/councilnews/pages/default.aspx?NewsID=510. Accessed 19 July 2013.

The National Archives (2013) 'Ministry of Health and Ministry of Labour, Later Ministry of Labour and National Service: Commissioners for Special Areas, Later Development Areas, Registered Files (DA, F and 99,000 Series)', Ref: MH 61. Available at: http://discovery.nationalarchives.gov.uk/SearchUI/Details?uri=C10904. Accessed 10 May 2013.

Osmond, J. (1977) *Creative Conflict*. Llandysul and London: Gomer Press and Routledge & Kegan Paul.

Osmond, J. (2008) 'Introduction', in Osmond, J. (ed.), *Futures for the Heads of the Valleys*. Cardiff: Institute of Welsh Affairs. 3–11.

Page, A. C. (1976) 'State Intervention in the inter-war period: the Special Areas Acts 1934–37', *British Journal of Law and Society*, 3(2), 175–203.

Tewdwr-Jones, M. (2002) *The Planning Polity: Planning, Government and the Policy Process*. London: Routledge.

University of Glamorgan (2012) *Merthyr Tydfil College Ltd Strategic Plan: 'Raising Aspirations and Maximising Potential' 2012/13–2015/16*. Pontypridd: University of Glamorgan.

WEFO (2013) *Map of the Convergence Area*. Available at: http://wefo.wales.gov.uk/programmes/convergence/areamap/?lang=en. Accessed: 16 May 2013.

Welsh Office (1967) *Wales: The Way Ahead*. Cardiff: HMSO.

The Works (2007) *Green Light for the Works*. Available at: http://www.theworksebbwvale.co.uk/home/news/green-light-for-the-works.aspx. Accessed: 17 March 2014.

The Works (2013a) *The Vision*. Available at: http://www.theworksebbwvale.co.uk/home/the-vision.aspx. Accessed: 18 July 2013.

The Works (2013b) *The Masterplan*. Available at: http://www.theworksebbwvale.co.uk/home/the-vision/the-masterplan.aspx. Accessed: 18 July 2013.

The Works (2013c) *State-of-the-art Learning Zone gets Official Opening*. Available at: http://www.theworksebbwvale.co.uk/home/news/state-of-the-art-learning-zone-gets-official-opening.aspx. Accessed: 17 March 2014.

Welsh Assembly Government (2002) *A Winning Wales: The National Economic Development Strategy of the Welsh Assembly Government*. Cardiff: Welsh Assembly Government.

Welsh Assembly Government (2004) *People, Places, Futures: The Wales Spatial Plan*. Cardiff: Welsh Assembly Government. Available at http://gov.wales/topics/planning/development-plans/wales-spatial-plan/?lang=en. Accessed: 19 May 2011.

Welsh Assembly Government (2005) *'Heads – We Win …' A Strategic Framework for the Heads of the Valleys*. Cardiff: Welsh Assembly Government.

Welsh Assembly Government (2006) *Turning Heads: A Strategy for the Heads of the Valleys 2020*. Cardiff: Welsh Assembly Government.

Welsh Assembly Government (2008) *People, Places, Futures: The Wales Spatial Plan 2008 Update*. Cardiff: Welsh Assembly Government.

5   East, west and the bit in the middle

Localities in north Wales

Robin Mann and Alexandra Plows

Introduction

This chapter examines ways of understanding and knowing north Wales, which in this instance, constitutes the six local authorities from Wrexham in the east, through Flintshire, Denbighshire, Conwy, Gwynedd, to Anglesey in the west. It encompasses the coastline of north and north west Wales, Snowdonia National Park and deep rural areas to the south of the locality. In particular, it is linked by the A55 trunk road from Chester to Holyhead docks; but with a large, less accessible hinterland away from the coastal A55 corridor (see Figure 5.1). We outline some of the key ways in which different parts, or localities, within north Wales are seen to connect or relate to each other. We examine different ways of constructing north Wales, for example, as divided by a rural north west and industrial north east, as linked by transport connections, and as cross-bordered. We consider how these situated understandings of locality shape, and are shaped by, specific factors including demographic changes and mobilities, economic and community regeneration as well as questions concerned with national identity and the Welsh language. This endeavour is based on a number of data collection exercises, including a baseline audit of available secondary data; interviews and focus groups with local governmental organisations as part of the WISERD stakeholder interview series; and small-scale qualitative fieldwork.

Linking north Wales: the A55 corridor

> There are two challenges in north Wales, one is sort of bridging east and west and I think also the other one is bridging from the A55 to the rural areas in the south.[1]

The above stakeholder sets an economic challenge for north Wales and the A55 appears central to this. In this context, the A55 is related to concerns about a lack of economic mutuality across north Wales, such that developments in the industrialised areas of the north east do not 'grasp' rural areas of the north west. Running 'east to west' from Chester to Holyhead docks, the A55 epitomises the

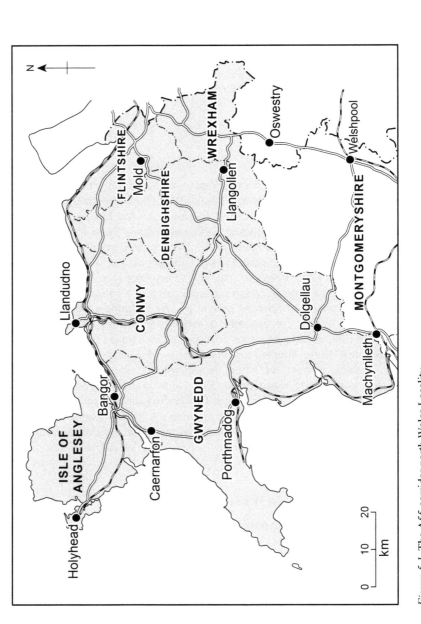

Figure 5.1 The A55 corridor north Wales Locality

Source: Mastermap Laver@Crown Copyright/database right 2010.

significance that is often placed on the cross-border relationship between north Wales and the north west of England (for a background to the economic rationales behind the A55 see Bryan et al., 1997, and Welsh Economy Research Unit, 1996). Starting in 1969, the A55 has developed through a series of road improvements, some of which were major infrastructure projects, the total cost of which has previously been estimated as in excess of £1 billion (Bryan et al., 1997: 227). The Welsh Assembly Government (WAG) *National Transport Plan* (2010) states that:

> the efficiency of the east–west corridor is of crucial importance to the future development of north Wales. Internal connectivity within north Wales is complex, but crucial to ensuring the distribution of growth and access to services and leisure.
>
> (Welsh Assembly Government, 2010: 31)

This account is corroborated by the following tourism stakeholder, who highlights the impact of increased connectivity for north west Wales:

> The A55 was a great investment … Post A55, what we have picked up is that there's kind of a shift by the customer who was saving 30 minutes in travel time; in actual fact [this] didn't make his journey time shorter, he spent the 30 minutes travelling further west … And I think that may have accelerated, you know, the Western periphery to be more popular.

As a site the A55 corridor cuts across administrative boundaries, covering six unitary authorities (if one includes Wrexham). It comprises a mixture of different contexts including: environmental (urban and rural); economic (e.g. deindustrialisation, farming, tourism, declining coastal resorts, numerous business parks and industrial estates); deprivation (areas having some of the least and most deprived districts in Wales) and language/cultural identity (areas of both high and low proportions of Welsh speakers, areas of significant in- and out-migration and cross-border relationships, as well as a notable migrant worker population in Wrexham).

Given this heterogeneity and diversity, proximity/distance to the A55 thus becomes a way of understanding 'micro-locality' differences within the north Wales 'site'. For example, access to the A55 means that you can reach the border and Chester within one hour when driving from locations east of Bangor. So, in understanding the multiple micro-localities of which north Wales is comprised, one key issue was to think about the differences between the coastal strip running parallel to the A55 and inland to the south. We can think about roads here as tributaries off the A55, so we have Holyhead–Llangefni and north to WYLFA nuclear power station and Amlwch; Bangor-Caernarfon–Llanberis; Llandudno–Llanrwst; Rhyl–Denbigh etc.

At the local authority level, both Anglesey and Gwynedd are 'rural' while the other north Wales authorities can be described as 'semi-rural'. At a lower scale, however, there is a mixed pattern of urban and fringe areas, small towns, villages and rural areas. A central feature of north Wales, therefore, is of a locality in which the rural is mingled with the urban, including several former slate-quarrying and coal-mining villages, as well as larger coastal conurbations whose viability is, at least in part, dependent on the recreational appeal of their rural hinterlands. A further related aspect to this understanding of micro-localities is the distinction between rurality and peripherality (Welsh Rural Observatory, 2007), and a perception of increasing peripherality as one moves from east to west. For instance, towns such as Caernarfon and Bangor are not rural but are characterised by a feeling of being peripheral, while nevertheless playing important roles for the populations they serve. A Welsh Rural Observatory report (2007) focuses on the unique make-up and role of such smaller-size towns in Wales which serve large rural areas. A related issue is the importance of scale and relativity when considering how concepts such as 'rural' are understood, and by whom; for example, those living in Caernarfon may not see themselves as rural, but may see other places within ten miles (such as villages on the Llyn Peninsula) as being rural. However, from the perspective of someone living in Wrexham, Caernarfon may seem extremely rural indeed.

A further important consideration was the need to account for localities in both north west and north east Wales. The Wales Spatial Plan (see Chapter 2 and below), for example, distinguishes between north west and north east and this distinction has historical, cultural and political resonance. Towards the north east are coastal towns such as Colwyn Bay, Rhyl, Prestatyn, Flint, Shotton. But away from the coast there are parts of north east Wales which are largely rural, characterised by village communities, with the area west of Wrexham becoming 'deep rural' (Welsh Rural Observatory, 2009). Wrexham itself is the largest town in north Wales and the fourth largest in Wales after Cardiff, Swansea and Newport.

Relationships with England: economy, mobility and identity

The A55 corridor also affords consideration of the extent to which localities across north Wales are embedded in different kinds of relationships with England. A distinctive aspect of north Wales, and of north east Wales in particular, is its cross-border relationship with England. Of all the Welsh regions, north Wales attracts the highest net number of migrants from England, with most migrants to Wales from England coming from north west England (Office for National Statistics, 2006). Compared to the rest of Wales, north Wales also has the highest net inflow of migrants aged 65+ as well as the highest net outflow of migrants to England aged 16–24. This would include students and graduates who move around the UK to university and to pursue careers.

These relationships, however, can be considered not only in terms of migration to and from England, but also more broadly in terms of mobilities, or people's daily movements. Certain places are embedded in cross-border relationships, particularly between Flintshire and the neighbouring English local authorities. Table 5.1 shows the percentage of 16–74-year-olds in employment who work in England. Over one in ten of those living in north Wales (11.4 per cent) travel to

Table 5.1 Living in Wales, working in England

Place of residence	16–74-year-olds in employment who work in England	
	%	Number
Flintshire	24.0	16,644
Wrexham	15.3	8700
Denbighshire	7.1	2697
Conwy	4.7	2054
Gwynedd	3.1	1439
Isle of Anglesey	2.6	680
North Wales	11.5	32,214
Wales	5.4	63,764

Source: Census 2001.

work in England. This is more than double the national Wales percentage (5.4 per cent). Furthermore, as many as 24 per cent of those living in Flintshire have their workplace across the English border.

This economic embeddedness between north east Wales and north west England is also reflected in the Spatial Plan for north east Wales in which economic regeneration is centred on the fostering of cross-border economic and business partnerships. Furthermore, the 2001 Census data on travel to work indicates that the numbers of people living in north west Wales and working in north east Wales vastly outweighs the opposing movements of people living in the north east and working in the north west. Conversely, one can think of opposing movements from east to west Wales when one considers recreational and leisure flows created by Snowdonia National Park and other opportunities. The 'tourism flow', as picked up by our previous tourism stakeholder, from east to west, and indeed from parts of England to the north west, is further emphasised when we consider that the dominant visitor sourcing areas to north Wales are the north west of England (37 per cent) and west Midlands (27 per cent) (north Wales Tourism Partnership, 2010). Patterns of east–west migration flow can also be examined by looking at 2001 Census data on country of birth (Figure 5.2).

Figure 5.2 shows the percentage of people born in the UK, outside of Wales, for local areas across north Wales. There are numerous districts where the non-Welsh-born population make up over 41 per cent of the population. The non-Welsh-born percentage in these areas is almost double the national Wales picture, where around a quarter of the Welsh resident population was born outside of Wales in the UK. In Flintshire, as in other unitary authorities close to the border, these figures are accentuated due to births in hospitals across the English border (this feature is also noted in the central Wales locality in Montgomeryshire). Yet there are also notable pockets of non-Welsh-born people in remote parts of Anglesey and south west of Gwynedd. A number of trends might be underlying these patterns such as the settlement of in-migrant families and retirees; welfare migration driven by a relative lower cost of living to certain

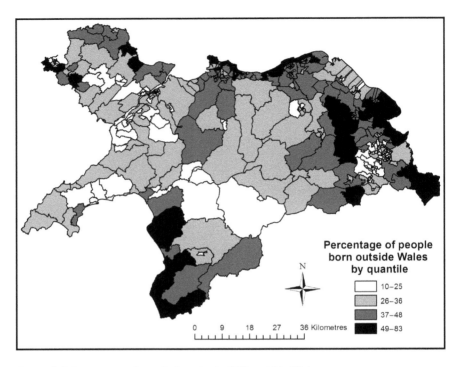

Figure 5.2 Percentage of people born in the UK, outside Wales

Source: Census 2001.
Contains National Statistics data © Crown copyright and database right 2012.
Contains Ordnance Survey data © Crown copyright and database right 2012.

parts of north Wales; and Flintshire as a commuting area for those working in England. The accentuation of these percentages due to births in hospitals in England is unlikely to influence percentages of non-Welsh born in Anglesey and Gwynedd.

Of course, these relationships can be contrasted to other places, where it is evident that networks and relationships remain largely locality-specific and often extend only to the nearest large town. This appears to be the case in the slate-mining villages on the western face of Snowdonia, which have historically looked, and continue to look, towards Caernarfon. Our qualitative research in these areas reports perceptions of being on 'the other side of the mountains' to the A55. Topographical landscapes are experienced as an important geographical boundary which has cultural and social implications. Both Caernarfon and Bangor represent major public sector employers (for example, Gwynedd County Council and the Countryside Council for Wales), as well as being sites of Welsh-language cultural and media industries. Smaller villages in the north west may be viewed simply as travel to work areas to these centres.

Interesting and policy-relevant questions would then be to understand the sense of participation and attachment of those people who have moved to live in Wales and their sense of identification with Wales compared with their place of origin (see, for example, Day et al., 2006). Table 5.2 shows the varying senses of national identity and Welsh-language ability across north Wales.

The table shows national identity options in terms of whether people report themselves as Welsh, British and/or English. These are not forced choices, but may also represent dual or multiple national identities.[2] Comparing these figures with the Welsh national average, a number of patterns can be discerned. First, the percentage reporting a Welsh national identity is higher in majority Welsh-speaking authorities of Gwynedd and Anglesey. But it is also high in Wrexham, close to the border, and where the percentage of Welsh speakers is similar to the Wales average. There is no simple east–west picture here. Substantial sections of the population do report themselves as British, and very likely as Welsh and British. Both British and English national identities run in the opposite direction. Reporting an English national identity is particularly high in Flintshire. Being born in Wales appears to make a significant difference to whether one reports oneself as Welsh. Of course, whether country of birth is an accurate indicator of anything can be debated. Yet, looking only at those born in Wales, there is much less variance in Welsh national identity across north Wales and in relation to Wales as a whole. In addition, is the varying significance of the Welsh language for national identity. In Gwynedd and Anglesey, most of the locally born population are Welsh speakers, with in-migrants making up most of the non-Welsh speaking population. In these areas, language may function as a significant marker of national identity and local/in-migrant status. In other local authorities, one finds that much of the locally born population do not speak Welsh, and so language is less likely to represent such an identity marker.

Finally, there appears to be a strong correlation between Welsh identity and the ability to speak Welsh. The suggestion from the data is that the majority of people reporting a Welsh national identity across north Wales are those who can speak

Table 5.2 National identities and Welsh-language ability in north Wales

Area	% Welsh	% British	% English	% Welsh-born national identity Welsh	% speak Welsh	% speak Welsh
Gwynedd	63.9	29.6	10.9	89.3	71.8	91.1
Wrexham	59.5	30.9	12.3	83.5	17.6	22.9
Isle of Anglesey	58.0	33.7	12.7	85.8	62.2	84.2
Denbighshire	48.6	37.7	17.8	79.2	31.1	45.4
Conwy	46.1	42.2	15.2	79.9	34.1	54.0
Flintshire	43.0	43.0	18.5	78.1	26.3	35.3
Wales	65.0	31.3	9.3	84.8	25.6	30.7

Source: Annual Population Survey, 2010.

Welsh. This trend is even evident in Flintshire, where Welsh identification is particularly low. The exception is Wrexham, a case of divergence between speaking Welsh and Welsh identity and where the pattern is similar to the national picture. It is also interesting that in Gwynedd, and to a lesser extent in Anglesey, the proportion of people who say they can speak Welsh is higher than those considering themselves as being Welsh. As discussed in Chapter 3, this can be contrasted to some authorities in south Wales (such as Blaenau Gwent or Merthyr Tydfil) where Welsh identity is around 80 per cent and Welsh-language ability is very low. Thus the relationship between national identity and Welsh-language ability presents itself in complex ways. In north Wales, at least, it would appear 'British' does not necessarily mean 'not Welsh'.

North Wales and spatial planning

Notions of north Wales, north east Wales and north west Wales can be invoked to express both social and economic coherences as well as incoherence. Such notions are also institutionalised through their correspondence to administrative boundaries and visions of regional working across these 'hard' local authority boundaries. Within the Welsh policy context, a key document has been the Wales Spatial Plan (Welsh Assembly Government, 2008) which states the Welsh government's vision for regional working across local authorities, private and third sectors. The Wales Spatial Plan distinguishes between north west Wales and north east Wales.[3] The north west Wales plan describes a natural and physical environment as well as a cultural and knowledge-based economy which supports a strong Welsh-language culture. Lack of opportunities for young people and the sustainability of Welsh-speaking communities receive specific attention. Equally, the area is seen to attract people for tourism and recreation, as well as offering quality of life that can lead to permanent settlement. Gwynedd and Anglesey play a key role in the north west Wales Spatial Plan. This interface between long-standing Welsh-speaking and in-migrant communities reflects the rural yet hybrid nature of the region.

Of key importance in the plan is the 'Menai hub' incorporating Bangor, Caernarfon and Llangefni. This includes significant cultural and knowledge-based economies such as those centred on Countryside Council for Wales, Bangor University and Welsh-language media industries. In Anglesey, there are two focuses of attention; southern Anglesey, which is included in the Llangefni, Bangor and Caernarfon hub, and north west Anglesey which is focused on the Holyhead hub. The Holyhead hub is defined as an area of national connectivity reflecting its importance as one of the main UK links to Dublin and Eire. Holyhead is also a key primary settlement and a key regeneration and key business sector area, as is Llangefni. Currently, Llangefni is the administrative centre for the island and houses the main council offices. The placing of the town within the Bangor hub seems rather strange therefore, perhaps implying that Llangefni should have a dual role. Interestingly, no Anglesey town is classed as being of key national importance, with Bangor being the only settlement in north west

Wales identified as such. This is despite the fact that Llangefni on Anglesey, and Caernarfon in Gwynedd, are core administrative centres, home not only to council offices but also magistrates' courts. Caernarfon is also a World Heritage site. It is worth noting that links from Anglesey to other areas in Wales are not identified. Anglesey is presented as being an important link to Dublin and Eire, as being part of the Caernarfon and Bangor hub, but not as having important links to other areas of Wales. Anglesey airport has only been in operation since 2007 so its impact on links to south Wales and Cardiff in particular remain to be assessed. However, the WAG *National Transport Plan* (2010) notes that:

> the existing intra-Wales air-service provides fast, efficient and reliable transport between north and south Wales. The service has proved extremely popular with passengers.
>
> (Welsh Assembly Government, 2010: 25)

The *National Transport Plan* aims to 'increase the capacity of the intra-Wales air service', although there have been significant teething problems.[4] Tourism on the island is confined to the coast, with only coastal areas being identified as Areas of Outstanding Natural Beauty and of having tourism potential. It is significant that the area covered by the central Wales Spatial Plan is depicted as 'extending' into the north west Wales Spatial Plan, particularly the southern Gwynedd region of Meirionydd, and extending up the Conwy Valley as far as Llanrwst. This crossover in the north west and central Spatial Plans is explicitly framed in terms of 'fuzzy boundaries' (Welsh Assembly Government, 2008), this 'fuzziness' reflecting inter-connectivity between north west and central Wales, especially regarding shared experience of the 'deep rural' (Welsh Rural Observatory, 2009). The farming heartland town of Bala, located in southern Gwynedd, exemplifies this 'fuzziness', identified in both the north west Wales and central Wales plans as a 'cross-boundary settlement'.

In some contrast to north west Wales, the north east Wales plan is described as a highly industrialised cross-border area. Central to the plan is the Wrexham–Deeside–Chester hub, which is distinct from the north coastal belt towns as well as the rural hinterland surrounding Llangollen. It is evident from the plan that cross-border linkages have particular importance to the economic prosperity of this area.

The plan considers the Wrexham hub to be distinct from the coastal belt towns of Rhyl, Prestatyn and others, as well as from the rural hinterland which includes Llangollen. It is evident from the Spatial Plan that cross-border linkages are viewed as crucial to the economic prosperity of this area (although it is also evident that this raises issues relating to identity, culture, community and language as a result of significant economic in-migration). There are questions as to whether this relationship amounts to inter-dependency as well as a tension between an 'all-Wales' focus and its pulls from outside. The high levels of economic in-migration can also be contrasted to net out-migration of young people aged 16–24. The north east Wales area and Wrexham, in particular, is highly dependent on the manufacturing sector, which makes it particularly susceptible to global economic changes. It also raises issues about the skills base of the local population for a knowledge economy, which is reflected in the lack of graduate employment opportunities in the area. Although there has been some success in redeveloping the area along the lines of high skills manufacturing, Wrexham and Flintshire are still structurally weaker than Chester in this respect.

Local perspectives and contested localities

'Place shaping' has become a term commonly adopted across UK government policy where there is an agreement on the importance of place in delivering (spatial) policy (Lyons Inquiry, 2007). However, places are constructed by people and hence perceptions and constructions of place (localities) vary. Different institutions, groups and individuals have different ideas of where place *is* and where boundaries and borders are; and also why and how place is important. Localities are often political constructs. Questions can thus be posed as to how new forms of spatial planning, as described above, are shaping the way stakeholders in north Wales understand the spaces for which they are responsible (in geographical and/or policy terms, or otherwise) and the ways in which they view themselves as being enabled or constrained to act within such shaped places. In some cases, there is evidence that the Spatial Plans are reflective of existing knowledge and identity claims about a region; in other cases, it would seem as if the Spatial Plans are 'place shaping' in new and contested ways.

The policy spaces of the localities in north Wales

How different stakeholders relate to the Spatial Plan can thus vary; interviews with stakeholders working in local government and in public bodies across the region suggest there may be important differences in these understandings of place in different parts of north Wales.

Figure 5.3 shows the spatial ellipses created from mapping the stakeholder interviews by seven policy themes. This reveals that the spatial focus of the stakeholders' working activities that emerged from the interviews generally go beyond the Wales Spatial Plan areas for north Wales and the A55 corridor focus of the north Wales Locality. The majority of ellipses are oriented north–south, reflecting the importance of Cardiff and the Welsh government in relation to policy areas. However, at least two policy themes (education and young people and crime, public space and policing) are oriented east–west, reflecting cross-border relations with England. Most of the ellipses are very similar in size and cover the same areas, suggesting an agreement in policy spaces in the locality, although the language, citizenship and identity ellipse and the education and young people ellipse are noted for their differences.

The areas common across all policies in terms of the core shared space and the spatial ellipse derived from all the stakeholder interviews are shown in Figure 5.4. The core area is focused on the Snowdonia National Park and the majority of

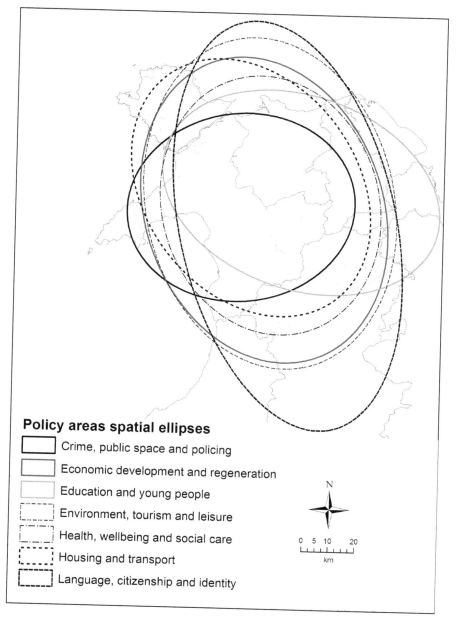

Policy areas spatial ellipses

Crime, public space and policing

Economic development and regeneration

Education and young people

Environment, tourism and leisure

Health, wellbeing and social care

Housing and transport

Language, citizenship and identity

N

0 5 10   20
km

Figure 5.3 Spatial ellipses of north Wales stakeholder interviews by policy area

Source: North Wales stakeholder interviews.
Contains Ordnance Survey data © Crown copyright and database right 2012.

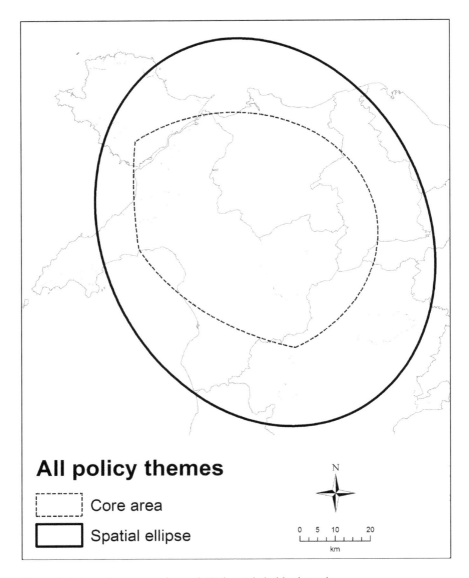

Figure 5.4 Areas in common in north Wales stakeholder interviews

Source: North Wales stakeholder interviews.
Contains Ordnance Survey data © Crown copyright and database right 2012.

Conwy. It hardly includes Anglesey or Wrexham and does not extend to the Welsh border. The ellipse is larger and encompasses the majority of north Wales and also north Powys, indicating the importance of links to south of the locality. These patterns are unpacked further with reference to individual stakeholders.

Isolated and self-orienting west?

Some of the issues and some of the problems of the western marginal areas haven't really changed for probably a long, long time. In some ways, it's worse because of the transportation and the service provision issues. There is a whole tranche of social economic transportation issues really, civil issues perhaps, and that hasn't changed. And it does tend to rely a lot on tourism, farming, obviously, in decline on behalf of the number of people employed and the rest of the farms being joined up. The loss of young skills, if you like, from the area, that's really a huge issue.

Particularly evident among stakeholders in Gwynedd was a tendency to define and describe their 'patch' in relation to its 'internal' nature, to its relative isolation and rurality. Below is an example of this rural, relatively inward-looking 'framing' from a housing stakeholder in Gwynedd, when asked to describe their geographical area of responsibility:

Geographically, I would say all of Gwynedd, it varies from rural to urban really. I mean there's a, quite, you know, very differing needs in different areas, you can imagine, Bangor, Caernarfon, I don't know how well you know the county but little villages and things as well further out, all totally different like Blaenau Ffestiniog, Dolgellau and, if you go down Tywyn, Barmouth which are holiday resorts. They're quite different. Bangor's a university town, Caernarfon, I suppose, is a tourist area. I have said, quite often in the past, you know we manage a housing estate down in Aberdyfi, well it would be a lot easier for me to get to Liverpool … than down to Aberdyfi.

In this specific example, Gwynedd is described in terms of the difference within different areas, ranging from urban to rural and those which are not easy to access. A related issue raised by one of our Gwynedd stakeholders was about space and the relatively large geographical size of the unitary authority (UA), and how this creates challenges for those responsible for maintaining partnerships and working in teams across the UA as a whole:

We've just given a presentation to the new Chief Executive of Public Health Wales … on 'What is Gwynedd, what is it like as a patch?', and we chose to lead on size … I just wanted to give this guy a sense of the size and the fact that it takes you two and a half hours to drive from one end of the patch to the other … the size is big and with a very small team thinly spread … some of the other teams work in one county … in the south in the valleys, for example, those counties can actually be very compact, you know they might have the same population as us … they can get around it … whereas we've got team members … it takes them an hour and a half to get here, to a team meeting so we never see them. So it's just a very different way of working.

The emphasis upon size by the above stakeholder can be seen as a general issue of rurality in two ways: first, because of the difficulty in travelling across the terrain and, second, because it has a sparse population.

Cross-bordered east

In contrast to the north west, several stakeholders in north east Wales positioned themselves in relation to the border with England, often referring to this as 'our larger geographical area' or 'our hinterland'.

> Everybody thinks of the A55 as linking north Wales, [but] it doesn't run through Wrexham, nor does the railway line and the north Wales Coast doesn't run through Wrexham, it's too far south ... So it's the A483 and we're more interested in the links to Shrewsbury as well ... And to the west Midlands, we're that little bit further south.

This quote comes from one of our Wrexham stakeholders talking about how Wrexham connects to other places, with an emphasis upon economic relationships and partnerships. This supports the *National Transport Plan* comments cited earlier, that internal connectivity in north Wales is 'complex'. This account of connectivity and 'flow' between north east Wales and north west England has implications for the Wales Spatial Plan, and economic partnerships such as Mersey Dee Alliance and north Wales Economic Forum. In this and other cases there is emphasis upon commonality with (north west) England. But this is clearly contested rather than assumed to be a shared way of thinking (e.g. 'I might be shot down on this by other people'; and below: 'there is a bit of tension for us') by those who may wish to stress or justify the Welshness of the authority. Moreover, we see a collapse of the local–national boundary through having adjacent authorities in England. While the border is invoked as a material entity, and ascribed with agency to influence policy delivery, it may be less salient for 'ordinary' residents who 'don't see the border' and who may even have a different national orientation:

> [T]here are some particular issues perhaps because we are so close to England and because a lot of the impact, you know, the economic impact on us is from England rather than from west Wales really.
>
>   I think one of the issues brought is our proximity to England really ... which is the thing that stands out for me because we are on the border of England ... And there's always an issue for us about, although we're part of Wales but we also have relationships with England. Erm, in terms of some regional planning issues. And also we tend to draw a lot of staff here from English areas. Like Cheshire, Merseyside, Manchester, Shropshire and so on. So I think being a border geographical area, in a border town, does have its own problems.

In contrast to the self-referential discourse among stakeholders in the north west, the north east Wales stakeholders describe their localities in terms of borders and flows. There are different borders and different sorts of flows across different sorts of borders:

> And I think in the north east, there's a lot of, still some ... industries there that are also a throwback to the past in some old-fashioned-type activities. And even there, there tends to be branch factories and they tend to be most vulnerable. And their staff might be people from across the border. And have issues in their economic way, because I think the, the value and the sort of hits that you get from an expenditure from a salary is where the person lives and not where the person works. So, erm, I think many of the businesses in the north east really benefit Merseyside more than it benefits the local area.

Linking west and east

> And one of the issues, I think, is how do we bridge between the north west and the north east. For example, I mean, if there are new jobs in the north east, what can we do to make them more attractive to people from the centre bits and the north west of Wales rather than from Merseyside. And I think the training bodies in Merseyside have been much more alive to, to these opportunities. If they knew there was a car plant coming to the north east of Wales, they would be up there training people and they'd be running buses from the Wirral down to Flintshire ... But us we don't seem to be quite so alive to what's happening. You know, and, I mean, it's only an hour and a bit from this part to Flintshire and people really travel a lot from those areas to work.

A number of issues are being raised here: first, that the bridging or linking of east and west is an economic problem – in particular, with regard to the need for the west to benefit from job creation in the east; second is the contrast between this lack of bridging, and Merseyside or England benefiting from jobs in the north east. A point is also being made about the greater ability of training bodies in Merseyside to identify and respond to employment opportunities. There is undoubtedly a national frame to this discourse which is about generating a west–east link, and contesting a north east Wales–England link. In contrast, the stakeholder below describes a different relationship between west and east related to access to services:

> If you live in Dolgellau and you'd want to take your wife to hospital or your husband to hospital you'd go to, guess where ... Where do you go? Wrexham ... And that's an awful long way if you've had a stroke ... Aberystwyth would be closer ... but their general hospital is Wrexham ... you know if you want to do a big shop, if you live in Dolgellau or one of those villages around Dolgellau, you know, you have to drive to Chester, um, Aberystwyth to an extent if you're happy with Morrison's but, um, you know, and most of them go to Chester or Wrexham. So the travel ... the travel areas are vast when you get in to the rural communities.

In this case there is a relationality here between north west (living in Dolgellau) and north east (travelling to hospital in Wrexham), albeit one not desired. As the stakeholder points out, southern parts of the north west, and northern parts of central Wales also look towards the east. Thus, there are different sorts of 'border flow' going on which we might characterise and differentiate as:

- *Affective flows*: shared spatial identities (e.g. cross-border, rural);
- *Pragmatic flows*: new rationalities; administrative boundaries dictating the direction of population flow across different local authority and national borders.

In the quote above, therefore, the stakeholder provides a narrative of a *pragmatic flow* from Dolgellau to Wrexham, rather than an *affective flow*. The implication is that Dolgellau and Wrexham do not form part of the same 'shared spatial'; the interviewee indicates that people in Dolgellau would 'naturally' turn west and south towards Aberystwyth for certain services, but instead are being asked to travel east. Policy and other changes can therefore give rise to what seem to be 'unnatural flows' where people are asked to shift towards thinking further afield to a different socio-spatial. This suggests that spatially orientated mentalities and historically established connections matter with regard to how people understand a particular spatial relationship; a journey might seem a long way, but if it is 'what we've always done', then this is a taken for granted, habituated norm, reflective of a shared spatial identity. People's perceptions of 'what works' with regard to policy flow thus relate to their concept of the locality. This is reflected in the Spatial Plans, with their emphasis on affective flow, the shared spatiality of the 'deep rural' in southern Gwynedd and mid/west Wales. But it also indicates ways in which flows between west and east result from practical policy relationships, but which may or may not be imagined or identified with by citizens themselves, at least initially:

> People in the west are more willing to travel than they used to because they've actually had to for the health services; for example, they have to travel, because the hospitals have been more sort of specialised now. Where people from our end have travelled to Glan Clwyd [hospital in north Wales], for example, whereas before they wouldn't and people are now much more willing to travel and it's easier for them to travel. I think there is a positive element there in some respects: people aren't so, quite so tied to their square mile as they used to be.

This stakeholder suggests a changing picture in which people are perhaps more willing to travel than previously because of new rationalities. Thus, new affective flows may develop over time as a result of policy changes which themselves become habituated, the new norm; these are localities in the process of co-construction.

North Wales

> Politically I think there is a feeling that there is a need for north Wales to speak with one voice. Some members do view that government working is centralised in Cardiff, probably more so than it's ever been ... some also feel that the politics behind the setting up of the Spatial Plan in north Wales ... [There's] also a tendency to split north Wales up into, well into two and a bit really, Spatial Plan areas ... that's a weakness at the moment in the current system because there's no mechanism that allows projects to be run on a pan-north Wales basis.

In the extract above, this economic stakeholder questions the logic of splitting north Wales into two Spatial Plans, arguing that 'thinking as a region' would be better for overall economic development. This again picks up the point that spatial 'place-shaping' may be seen or experienced as an imposition, rather than as reflecting 'common knowledge'. Again, it is likely that different domains/policy areas (and accruing forms of knowledge) – in this case, economic development – can understand place and space differently and hence have a different account of what would 'work' in terms of connectivity or contrast between regions, and in terms of their role and policy area. This has implications in terms of policy and strategy, as how a region is defined, where boundaries are drawn and how the needs of a region are understood can vary depending on the context. Different policy sectors, different goals and different knowledge bases all contribute to how 'north Wales' is defined and delineated. The same concerns about splitting north Wales into two (and a half) Spatial Plans are to the fore in this account from a tourism stakeholder, who brings his knowledge of his own sector (tourism) to bear on the issue of 'fuzzy boundaries' :

> From a tourism perspective we automatically think from a customer's viewpoint because the customer, visitor sees none of these boundaries and we try and harness those boundaries as appropriate whilst we've developed our most recent strategy, we have an overall action for north Wales we have got a chap that discusses the issues of the north west, discusses the issues of north east. Identifies the differences between those two Spatial Plans and then we have the two action plans so one says all these things in one shopping list and another. The line is not perfectly the same as a Spatial Plan. We see the north west Spatial Plan stopping just west of Llandudno ... but from a visitor perspective we think Llandudno is in the west. So, you know, that little wedge in the middle, our fuzzy line will include Llandudno in the west whereas the Spatial Plan would include Llandudno in the east. And I think if I look at the way the Spatial Plan is evolving, I think the Welsh Assembly Government is less sensitive about conformity with a highly precise boundary by now.

Place and community regeneration

Concepts of 'community' and 'community regeneration' are understood and operationalised differently within different places. This difference relates, in part at least, to differences in geography and demographic trends which affect how communities are understood (by policy-makers, community members, other stakeholders), and thus how community regeneration strategies are rolled out and responded to. Thus far, we have focused on baseline quantitative data as well as qualitative interviews with senior managers in local authorities and public bodies. In this section we turn our attention to the perspectives of local-level actors in the form of community workers and activists. Two sites are examined: a rural village in north west Wales and a deprived housing estate in Wrexham. The first is one of the former slate-mining villages to the south of the Snowdonia mountain range which historically look more towards Caernarfon, with high levels of Welsh speakers. The second is urban, situated close to the English border with historically high levels of in- and out-migration and population flow. Both are areas identified for Communities First funding, which since 2001 has been WAG's flagship community regeneration programme (see Welsh Assembly Government, 2007).

We identify that notions of community regeneration 'play out' differently in these localities. Through this focus, we illustrate the way that place, and its situatedness within a broader knowledge of locality, shapes the way individual capacity-building translates into community regeneration. What is of note is how patterns of mobility, as discussed in previous sections, have an impact on community regeneration, as is evidenced in the extract below by what was termed the 'churn effect':[5]

> [O]ne of the things that we're looking at now is an evaluation framework for our whole community regeneration programme ... we're looking at the impact on the individual with [our] local learning programme ... One of the things that buggers it up is the 'churn effect', so if you get that degree, you leave the area ... how do you prove that community economic development is effective and if it is worth investing [in]?

The suggestion here is that in areas where there is high mobility, such as north east Wales/Wrexham, the 'churn effect' may be more of a factor. Therefore, the experience of community regeneration in Wrexham, according to this stakeholder, is that individual capacity-building and up-skilling often leads to out-migration, which doesn't actually help the place itself (community capacity-building). Thus, there is a difference between understanding the 'success' of community regeneration as (a) individual capacity-building and (b) building the capacity of the place itself: community sustainability. An interview with a Gwynedd stakeholder, by contrast, indicated that individuals who built capacity in relation to regeneration used these acquired skills to develop community capacity:

> [C]ommunity development as in capacity-building ... Skills for, getting people involved in their communities ... people do develop themselves

into a voice for a certain group ... or to represent a certain issue in the communities ... but also to develop specific capital and revenue projects that meet a need.

These stakeholders thus provide interesting differences in their accounts of community regeneration. In Wrexham, individuals who have built capacity in the community regeneration area (skills, training) subsequently leave the area. In Gwynedd, those individuals who acquire skills do so seemingly from the outset with the explicit intention of staying put and using these skills for the benefit of their community. This focus on community regeneration as meaning community capacity-building is also expressed by those Gwynedd stakeholders tasked with delivering the regeneration programme – it is a conscious strategy. This may relate to the fact that Gwynedd is, as previously described, more 'self-orienting', and demographically does not experience the same levels of in- and out-migration as north east Wales does, as previous sections have demonstrated. Because of its lack of connectivity to other places, Gwynedd, therefore, draws more on a historical practice of sustaining and developing internal capacity – for example, preserving the Welsh language and halting the out-migration of young people. These practices can also be viewed as local political responses to wider economic development policies and their negative effects on north west Wales (see Lovering, 1983, and Williams, 1980, for such critiques). Hence, community regeneration is seen in these terms by local stakeholders and community members, as well as within the north west Spatial Plan.

The north Wales village pilot study also provided evidence of communities looking to themselves to develop and sustain capacity. In this interview extract below, a key local figure, provides a narrative of founding a long-standing not-for-profit community organisation focused on community and economic regeneration:

I was one of the instigators who formed [the company] ... I suggested that we invited somebody from the WDA to give us a talk about what plans they had for the valley. This guy came from Bangor and he told us that this was just a travel to work area and they hadn't got any plans, and it turned out into quite a row and I got asked to leave by the Chairman because I just couldn't understand how they could look at a valley which had had so much industrial involvement in the past could be ignored for any industrial development in the future. Following that I called a meeting of the Community Council, and had the members here, in my house, and I said 'Right, nobody's going to help us, we've got to form some kind of something to help ourselves.'

This narrative closely maps onto the north west region Spatial Plan, with regard to the identified need to sustain communities in areas experiencing the out-migration of young people post industrial closure. However, in relation to community capacity-building, this stakeholder goes on to say that:

> I'd say now that without the people who have moved in and that are taking part, hardly anything would happen here.

This is, firstly, identifying 'churn' of a sort; while not at the levels of in- and out-migration experiences on the north east borders, this village in western Snowdonia has experienced the out-migration of young people, and relatively modest levels of in-migration. Secondly, this account highlights that this narrative of 'self-sustaining communities' in north west Wales is, in fact, more accurately a narrative of localities which are significantly dependant on outside inputs (in-migrants). The pilot study further identified that while many in-migrants (who could be generalised as being middle-class English) were very keen to put down roots in their community, various divisions and differences in culture and outlook (class, language, insider/outsider status) were a stumbling block affecting uptake, mobilisation and capacity-building with relation to regeneration initiatives (see Mann et al., 2011). While a clear contrast can be made to the 'churned' status of community in the Wrexham example, it is also the case that north west Wales communities are not wholly 'self-sufficient', but, indeed, draw on outside inputs for community capacity-building and regeneration.

Conclusion

To what extent, and for whom, is north Wales a coherent socio-spatial form? Drawing these different evidence bases together, in what sense can one talk of an overall similar trend taking place across north Wales? Differences between north Wales localities – between west and east, for example – are perhaps more striking than the points of similarity and convergence. Parts of north east Wales are characterised by their embeddedness within a cross-border region. This is sometimes contested by those advocating the promotion of a north Wales economic region. But it does appear to be reflected in community regeneration strategies. Parts of north west Wales, particularly in the 'deep rural' away from the A55 coastal strip, could be described as less connected and less mobile, and focused on internal capacity-building – for example, having a strategic focus on community capacity-building where individual capacity is envisaged (and hence planned for) as feeding into broader community benefit.

Data on north east Wales suggests a high degree of interrelation with England, compared to other parts of Wales. The salience of these cross-border networks and ties would suggest that the border region of north east Wales is an appropriate location for considering the impact of policy divergence between England and Wales on the lives of ordinary people. In-depth qualitative research, in combination with survey research, would be needed in order to interrogate these relationships. The salience of these cross-border networks and ties would suggest that the border region of north east Wales is an appropriate location for considering the impact of policy divergence between England and Wales on the lives of ordinary people – for example, how living close to the border shapes their choices and decision-making with regard to access to services. Mobilities, and the limits of mobilities, need to be factored into place-based policies aimed at community regeneration and increasing educational and labour market opportunities. Strategies for community regeneration need to address the issue of what 'success' looks like, and of the translation of individual into community capacity-building.

Different goals, values and knowledge bases all contribute to how 'north Wales' is defined and delineated. For example, different knowledge bases embedded in various policy sectors (crime, housing, economic development) mean that people can understand place and space differently, and thus have a different account of what would 'work' in terms of connectivity or contrast between regions. This has implications for policy and strategy, for example, with regards to the uptake of the Spatial Plan, as how a region is defined, where boundaries are drawn and how the needs of a region are understood can vary depending on the context. In some circumstances, there is evidence that the Spatial Plans reflect existing knowledge and identity claims about a region and 'ways of doing things'; in other cases, it would seem as if the Spatial Plans are 'place-shaping' in new ways, which may not reflect existing localities but may come to reflect them over time. We have also identified that there are many different sorts of flow happening, across many different borders, and that the 'fuzzy boundaries' identified in the Spatial Plan are reflective of many shifting and fuzzy boundaries, as people negotiate across space and place in different circumstances. We have shown that 'the shared spatial' can account for what might be termed 'affective flows', for example, between mid and north Wales. Other flows are more pragmatic, catalysed by new types of policy delivery, such as the movement between Dolgellau and Wrexham to access health services. Over time, these may develop into new affective flows and develop a historical affective resonance of their own, reflective of new working and governance patterns.

Notes

1 We draw on data from the stakeholder interview series carried out as part of the WISERD Localities research programme. This comprised a number of interviews with senior personnel in local government and public bodies across selected local authority areas of Wales. For the purposes of this chapter we focus on the stakeholder interviews collected within the north west and north east Wales spatial plan areas.

2 The national identity question in Wales asks 'What do you consider your national identity to be? Please choose as many or as few as apply': 1. Welsh, 2. English, 3. Scottish, 4. Irish, 5. British, 6. Other answer. This quote is derived from the stakeholder interview programme. All subsequent quotes in this chapter are also taken from these interviews (unless otherwise stated).

3 The six 'area visions' of the Wales Spatial Plan are: central Wales; north east Wales (Border and Coast); north west Wales (Eryri a Môn); Pembrokeshire (The Haven); south east Wales (Capital Network); and Swansea Bay (Waterfront and Western Valleys).

4 Highland Airways, the company running the link, went into administration in March 2010 but the Anglesey–Cardiff air service link has continued following a WAG subsidy of £1.2 million, reflecting the strategic importance of the link for WAG (see BBC News, 2011).
5 Like attrition or turnover, churn refers to the number of individuals or things which move in or out of a collective over a period of time (see Department of Communities and Local Government, 2009).

References

BBC News (2011) *North–South Wales Air Service Subsidy Rises to 1.2 Million*. Available at: http://www.bbc.co.uk/news/uk-wales-11904955. Accessed 17 February 2015.

Bryan, J., Hill, S., Munday, M. and Roberts, A. (1997) 'Road infrastructure and economic development in the periphery: the case of A55 improvements in North Wales', *Journal of Transport Geography*, 5(4), 227–37.

Day, G., Davis, H. and Drakakis-Smith, A. (2006) 'Being English in North Wales: in-migration and the in-migrant experience', Nationalism and Ethnic Politics, 12(3–4), 577–98.

Department of Communities and Local Government (2009) *Population Churn and its Impact on Socio-economic Convergence in the Five London 2012 Host Boroughs*. London: DCLG.

Haselden, L. (2003) *Difference in Estimates of Welsh Language Skills*. Office for National Statistics. Available at: http://www.ons.gov.uk/ons/search/index.html?pageSize=50&sortBy=none&sortDirection=none&newquery=haselden. Accessed 17 February 2015.

Higgs, G., Williams, C. and Dorling, D. (2004) 'Use of the census of population to discern trends in the Welsh language', *Area*, 36(2), 187–201.

Lovering, J. (1983) 'Gwynedd: a county in crisis', Coleg Harlech, Occasional Papers in Welsh Studies, No. 2.

Lyons Inquiry (2007) *Place-shaping: A Shared Ambition for the Future of Local Government*. Available at: https://www.gov.uk/government/uploads/system/uploads/attachment_data/file/229035/9780119898552.pdf. Accessed 19 May 2015.

Mann, R., Plows, A. and Patterson, C. (2011) 'Civilising community? Local civil society in north west Wales: a critical exploration'. WISERD Working Paper.

North Wales Tourism Partnership (2010) *Tourism Strategy North Wales 2010–2015*. Available at: http://denbighddms.wisshost.net/webfiles/submission/CD%202/LDP%20Evidence%20Base%20EB%20(August%202011)%20Part%20II/EB027%20Tourism%20Strategy%20North%20Wales.pdf. Accessed 30 April 2015.

Office for National Statistics (2006) *Patterns of Migration in Wales*. London: ONS.

Welsh Assembly Government (2007) *Communities First Guidance 2007*. Cardiff: Welsh Assembly Government.

Welsh Assembly Government (2008) *People, Places, Futures: The Wales Spatial Plan*. Cardiff: Welsh Assembly Government.

Welsh Assembly Government (2010) *National Transport Plan*. Cardiff: Welsh Assembly Government.

Welsh Economy Research Unit (1996) *Delivering the Goods? The Economic Impact of A55 Expressway Improvements*. British Road Federation, March.

Welsh Rural Observatory (2007) *Small and Market Towns in Rural Wales and their Hinterlands*. Research Report 13. Available at: http://www.walesruralobservatory.org.uk/sites/default/files/Market%2520Towns%2520report%2520final2.pdf. Accessed 17 February 2012.

Welsh Rural Observatory (2009) *Deep Rural Localities*. Available at: http://www. walesruralobservatory.org.uk/sites/default/files/DeepRuralReport_Oct09_0.pdf. Accessed 17 February 2012.

Williams, G. (1980) 'Industrialisation, inequality and deprivation in rural Wales', in Rees, G. and Rees, T. (eds), *Poverty and Social Inequality in Wales*. London: Croom Helm. 168–84.

6   Locating the mid Wales economy

Jesse Heley, Laura Jones and
Suzie Watkin

Introduction

This chapter concerns itself with interrogating the multiple, sometimes contested, ways of knowing, narrating and locating contemporary mid Wales as a political-economic context, and its contingent social relations. This analysis proceeds through the specific spatial lens of what we term the Central and west Coast Locality (CWCL); an area arcing across central Wales and the south west seaboard, extending from St David's Head to the Shropshire border and from the Preseli Mountains and Teifi Valley to the Berwyn range and the River Dyfi (see Figure 6.1). The landscape of the CWCL is regarded as broadly and predominantly rural, with no town in this locality having a population of more than 17,000 people.

At the same time, this area has the potential to provide insights into the ongoing processes of economic restructuring and differentiation occurring across the Welsh countryside (see Day et al., 1989), as the declining dominance of agricultural employment has given rise to new modes of economic, social and political relations (Marsden et al., 1993; Marsden, 1998). The CWCL has thus witnessed the spatially variable growth and rise to prominence of different economic sectors (e.g. public sector, tourism and hospitality services, and energy production) in relation to the particular local factors and conditions encountered across parts of this broadly rural locality. This is not to suggest that agriculture is no longer significant – with its continuing not only as an important economic practice, but also occupying a central role in social and cultural understandings of place – rather that mid Wales as an economic space is becoming increasingly complex. This presents policy-makers and local residents with ongoing economic challenges and opportunities through increased interconnections with national and international markets.

In contrast then, with the localities of the Heads of the Valleys and the A55 corridor (see chapters 4 and 5), which have variously been defined in regard to their contemporary and past industrial functions, mid Wales is an area which is hard to grasp as having an overarching economic character. Instead, the notion of mid Wales being a specifically 'rural' economy as variously defined, and with associated capacities and vulnerabilities, provides a form of spatial cohesion in

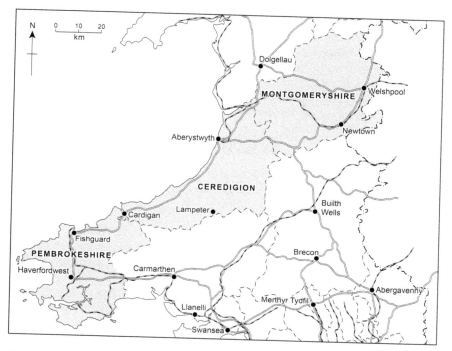

Figure 6.1 The Central and West Coast Locality

Source: Mastermap Layer@Crown Copyright/database right 2010.
An Ordnance Survey/EDINA supplied service.

the imaginative and material practices of policy-makers and local economic actors. While processes of social and economic restructuring and associated demographic changes have led to the analytical value of the 'rural' as a spatial category being called into question (Hoggart, 1990), it is clear that the rural continues to retain a powerful meaning to many people. In this way, rural space has come to be understood not only on the basis of the material conditions in particular localities, but as a composite of place, representation and lived experience (see Halfacree, 2006). As Woods explains in reference to these three 'portals':

> The portal of 'rural locality' allows us to glimpse the structural patterns produced by specific configurations of larger social and economic processes; the portal of 'representations of the rural' provides sight of the discursive meanings applied to the rural in relation to the wider world; and the portal of 'everyday lives of the rural' illuminates the routine enactment of a relational rural by individuals whose mobility is not constrained to rural space.
>
> (2011: 292)

In this chapter, we consider how these three intertwined facets have been used to locate mid Wales as a *rural economic space*. Specifically, we consider how the notion of mid Wales as a rural locality with particular economic capacities, opportunities and vulnerabilities has been variously understood and re-presented through national policy discourses of regional development and by local economic actors in relation to the context of economic recession. These under-standings in turn have material effects in rural localities, as they shape the every-day experiences of people who live, work and play in the CWCL.

The Central and West Coast Locality

> Mid Wales is still a very traditional part of Wales ... it hasn't experienced the economic boom that the city would have experienced down in the south, the M4 belt of Swansea and Cardiff.[1]

The territory we refer to as the Central and West Coast Locality (CWCL) includes the former counties of Powys and Dyfed, but our discussion focuses primarily on the administrative areas of Pembrokeshire and Ceredigion. This is in keeping with our data collection process, whereby stakeholder interviews were primarily undertaken with people working in these locations. Aberystwyth, Haverfordwest, Milford Haven and Newtown are the largest population centres, but the settlement pattern is overwhelmingly that of small market towns, with the locality being accordingly fractured into multiple labour markets and catchment areas for shopping and services. The CWCL boasts an outstanding natural environment, encompassing the Dyfi UNESCO Biosphere area, the Pembrokeshire Coast National Park, the Ceredigion Heritage Coast and the Cambrian Mountains, each important both to conservation and biodiversity, and to tourism and recreation.

The CWCL exists in various relational contexts which can be approached from cultural, social, political and economic perspectives. Culturally and socially the locality is surprisingly diverse, with strong 'indigenous' identities in each of the three counties. This is particularly so in Ceredigion, where a significant propor-tion of the population identify themselves as 'Cardis', while Montgomeryshire maintains an historic 'Mont' identity. The strength of the Welsh language decreases along a gradient from west to east and north to south, with traditional Welsh-language heartlands in Ceredigion, northern Pembrokeshire and western Montgomeryshire giving way to the historically anglicised district of south Pembrokeshire and the anglicised border country of Montgomeryshire (see Davies, 2006). The prevalence of the Welsh language in its traditional heartlands has, however, been weakened by in-migration, especially in coastal areas, although this has in turn been offset by the revitalisation in the medium of Welsh over the last 30 years, driven largely by the political shift in education policy and the consequent rise of the Welsh language in the classroom (Jones-Evans et al., 2011). Certainly, mid Wales has historically differentiated itself politically within Welsh national context and the struggle both for and against the Welsh language has played a significant part in this process. But this is only part of the story. In their highly regarded study of Cardiganshire in the early 1970s, P. J. Madgwick et al. (1973) painted a picture of rural mid Wales which identified a very particular and radical element in the political scene. This account gave voice to a distinct class structure within the community, which, along with non-conformism in religious traditions, was shaped by the lived experience of the often-harsh agricultural conditions of the area.

Put in historical context, mid Wales is (or certainly was) strongly non-conformist and levels of church or chapel attendance were comparatively high in the early to mid-twentieth century (ibid.). This condition is closely allied to what might be understood as Welsh culture, and bound up with moral and cultural mores, and formal political activity. In particular, mid Wales served as an important backdrop for Liberalism, and the Liberal Party held the Cardiganshire seat continuously between 1880 and 1966, as well as having strong support in Montgomeryshire, holding the seat from 1880 to 1979. In more recent times, however, the political scene has been much more tentative, with Plaid Cymru, the Conservatives and Labour all enjoying varying proportions of the vote in the counties of the CWCL, alongside continued support for the now Liberal Democrats among a large swathe of residents.

As a whole, the locality has an expanding population and this is in stark contrast to the mid-twentieth century when the mid Wales region, including Ceredigion and Montgomeryshire, had the severest rate of population decline in Britain. There are still, however, pockets of depopulation, especially in northern and south west Pembrokeshire. Similarly, a relative overall level of prosperity disguises severe pockets of deprivation, with wards in Pembroke and Pembroke Dock ranking among the 100 most deprived in Wales. Problems of deprivation and isolation are intensified for individual households by the poor transport infrastructure of the region; with accessibility to health care, schooling and other public and commercial services a major and ongoing issue in the locality.

Economically, the historic centrality of agriculture has been somewhat overtaken by the growth of the service sector. In western Pembrokeshire, the more urban, industrial economy of Milford Haven and Pembroke Dock has shifted in emphasis from fishing and shipping to oil and gas, forming one of Britain's major entry points for liquid natural gas. Towns such as Cardigan, Llanidloes and Welshpool were traditional centres for manufacturing, and Newtown was promoted as an industrial growth pole in the post-war era by the former Development Board for Rural Wales (which covered Ceredigion and Montgomeryshire) (see Day and Hedger, 1990). Rapid growth in manufacturing employment during the 1970s and 1980s has, however, been followed by deindustrialisation and factory closures, under pressure from international competition and a relative rise in production costs. The closure of clothing company Dewhirst's plants at Cardigan and Fishguard in 2002, for example, had a significant local impact, with the loss of over 300 jobs. Rural Wales was also hard hit by the foot and mouth outbreak in 2001, with devastating impacts on individual farm livelihoods as well as wider repercussions for the agri-food, tourism and recreation sectors of the economy (see Scott et al., 2004).

Yet the mid Wales economy as a whole was able to cope, with the locality's economic drivers now established as the administrative and service centres of Aberystwyth, Haverfordwest and Llandrindod Wells, and already high levels of public sector employment further supplemented by the relocation of several Welsh government departments and functions to new offices in Aberystwyth in 2010. These included Rural Affairs and Heritage, elements of the Department of Economy and Transport, and Sustainable Futures. Other regional provisions, such as translation and communication teams, were also transferred. The universities at Aberystwyth and Lampeter, and the National Library of Wales at Aberystwyth, are also important employers and cultural institutions. Ceredigion and Pembrokeshire are part of the west Wales and the Valleys Convergence Region, and have received substantial investment from the EU Structural Funds since 2000. Development programmes have supported innovation in the agri-food and tourism sectors, promoting a locally embedded 'eco-economy'. More recently, the particular status, capacity and potential of the mid Wales economy have been addressed as part of the national development strategy which is the Wales Spatial Plan (Welsh Assembly Government, 2004, 2008a).

Political context: the Wales Spatial Plan

The Wales Spatial Plan (WSP) is the Welsh Assembly governments' (WAGs') flagship strategy for sustainable development in dialogue with the challenges presented by population and economic change. Promoted as a 'vision' for increasing national competitiveness, the WSP is a regional model for improving accessibility, communications and social wellbeing, and for stimulating economic growth in all localities. This document fashions a set of coherences structured around six regional economies, each of which is identified as having particular economic conditions, and each of which requires a tailor-made response to the challenges posed by globalisation. These areas are: central Wales; north east Wales (Border and Coast); north west Wales (Eryri a Môn); Pembrokeshire (The Haven); south east Wales (Capital Network); and Swansea Bay (Waterfront and Western Valleys).

The CWCL is not coterminous with any one of the six areas mapped out by the WSP, and straddles The Haven and, to a much greater extent, central Wales. Taking each area in turn, the vision and priorities for The Haven as laid out in the WSP strongly reflect the importance of coastal activities as a driver for industrial and commercial growth. On this basis The Haven area plan makes much of the need for improving strategic transport links and economic infrastructure in order to fully exploit the potential of Pembrokeshire's maritime assets. This includes addressing the needs of the petro-chemical and fishing industries, as well as the tourism and leisure sectors where there is a strong desire to increase higher value-adding activities as a means of boosting the rural economy.

Central Wales is the largest Spatial Plan area by some margin, stretching from Snowdonia and southern Conwy and Denbighshire through Powys and Ceredigion into south west Wales. In contrast to The Haven, which has a clear sense of identity fashioned around promoting and developing a network of towns around the Haven Waterway, the personality of central Wales as defined in the WSP is much more oblique. Indeed, as Haughton et al. detail in their summary of the consultation process which informed the development of the 2008 Spatial Plan Update, central Wales was the 'one area that tended to be mentioned in the interviews as lacking any great functional cohesion' (2010: 146). Instead, the central Wales area was seen to 'represent the remaining parts of Wales after the other functional spaces had been identified' (ibid.). For Haughton et al. this linked to further criticisms aired during the consultation process regarding the Plan's failure to adequately grasp the breadth and complexity of rural issues at play in (central) Wales.

In light of these criticisms, in the 2008 Spatial Plan the central Wales area is represented as a distinct blend of environmental, social, cultural and economic characteristics whose 'intimate relationship, make [this area] the heartland of rural life and one of the storehouses of Wales ... particularly in terms of "environmental capital"' (Welsh Assembly Government, 2008a: 50). However, and despite efforts to better detail the 'blend' of rural life and build a strategy which adequately addresses the development needs of communities in the countryside, the extent to which this is incumbent in the current Spatial Plan remains open to question, and particularly in regard to questions of employment and the economy. This will be the focus of the remainder of this chapter, which uses secondary and primary data gathered in the CWCL to question the assumptions regarding mid Wales and rurality as the key binding feature in this space, as put forward in the Central WSP Area Strategy.

The policy spaces of the CWCL

The spatial ellipses derived from the stakeholder interview themes, shown in Figure 6.2, reveal a tight spatial focus across the eight policy areas compared to the other two localities. Nearly all of the ellipses share the same north east–south west orientation encompassing Ceredigion and the majority of Carmarthenshire and Pembrokeshire.

The two exceptions are language, citizenship and identity – which has a north–south orientation that does not include Pembrokeshire, possibly reflecting the lack of a strong Welsh-speaking community here – and economic development and regeneration, which has an east–west orientation focused on the south of the locality and taking in Swansea and the unitary authorities west of the valleys. The spatial focus of the stakeholder interviews on Ceredigion, Pembrokeshire and north and west Carmarthenshire is interesting as these cover the previous county of Dyfed – which vanished in 1996 when local government in Wales was reorganised – and perhaps reflect the ongoing legacy and influence of past administrative structures. It is also worth noting the lack of spatial focus on areas north of Ceredigion in any of the policy themes.

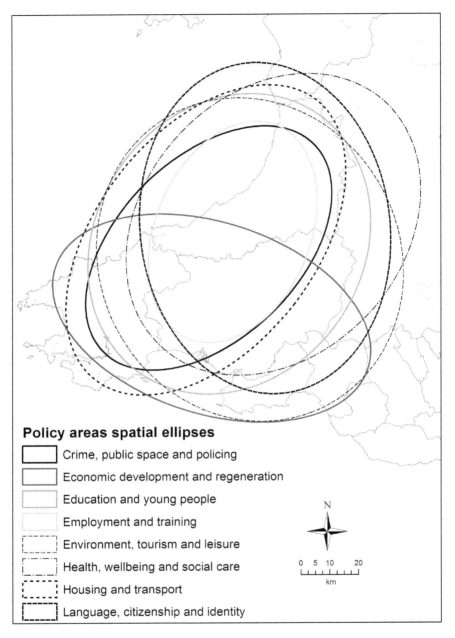

Figure 6.2 Spatial ellipses of CWCL stakeholder interviews by policy area

Source: CWCL stakeholder interviews.
Contains Ordnance Survey data © Crown copyright and database right 2012.

The common areas to stakeholders across all policy themes are illustrated in Figure 6.3. The core area that covers all the eight policy themes is fairly small and is concentrated in north west Carmarthenshire and includes the south part of Ceredigion and the north east edge of Pembrokeshire. This is the central area of the old Dyfed County Council and indicates that the old administrative ties and spatial focus of the former county council have a strong influence on the working

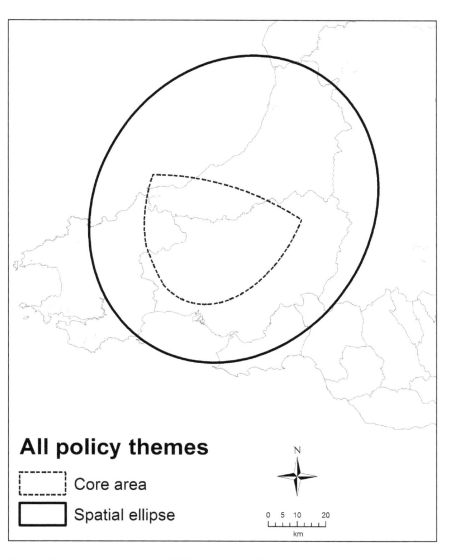

Figure 6.3 Areas in common in CWCL stakeholder interviews

Source: CWCL stakeholder interviews.
Contains Ordnance Survey data © Crown copyright and database right 2012.

activities of the stakeholders in CWCL, despite the fact that they are split across three unitary authorities. The spatial ellipse derived from all of the stakeholder interviews shows a much wider spatial focus that covers the majority of Ceredigion and Pembrokeshire but also includes the hinterland of Swansea.

The central Wales Spatial Plan area

The ambition for central Wales, according to the Wales Spatial Plan, is one of 'high quality living and working in smaller-scale settlements set within a superb environment, providing dynamic models of rural sustainable development, moving all sectors to higher value added activities' (Welsh Assembly Government, 2008a: 50). This developmental goal for central Wales is a framework response to a series of factors associated with rural economies and a low-density population, and which are largely cast in a negative light. These factors include a predominance of low wages, a restricted range of job opportunities, peripherality to major economic markets and a below-critical-mass level for investment in major communication improvements. More specifically, the needs of central Wales as defined/institutionalised by the WSP are grouped around the cross-cutting issues of communication, employment and labour markets, which are briefly and directly expanded upon below.

Communications: The Central WSP Strategy states a need to increase 'sustainable accessibility' of economic, commercial and knowledge markets within Wales, and at UK, European and global scales. At present, few areas have strong internal communication links (including those of information communication technologies [ICT]), with poor public transport and limited rail access. This results in a high dependency on private car ownership, which in turn exacerbates the issue of fuel poverty.

Employment: Central Wales has a relatively low level of unemployment, and this is ostensibly a positive feature. Nevertheless, the Spatial Plan suggests that this foreshadows a dependency on the public sector, and a below-average private sector which is dominated by small-scale enterprises. Such enterprises, it is maintained, have restricted opportunities to expand, given a limited consumer base. Furthermore, the region is stated as having underdeveloped ties between producers, suppliers and retailers, and this is particularly so in regard to agriculture, which continues to serve as an important element of the economy.

Labour market: The population of central Wales is relatively over-characterised by middle-aged and elderly residents. This is generally attributed to a quality-of-life pull, and poses immediate and long-term issues for health and social care provision. In respect to the working-age population, there is recognition of the barriers presented by limited transport, childcare and ICT infrastructures. Additionally, the preponderance of small urban settlements in the region is identified as providing insufficient economic opportunities to retain a population characterised by high levels of educational attainment. On a related point, the region is taken to have spatially restricted capacity for attracting highly qualified in-migrants – due to the presence of universities and various government departments. This is significant, perhaps, in that opportunities for highly qualified in-migrants are concentrated in a limited number of key service centres in the region.

In sum, the WSP sets out central Wales as a region, which, despite strong social and environmental credentials, has significant economic weaknesses. These weaknesses, in turn, are attributed to peripherality and the lack of effective internal and cross-border communications. This represents a dominant discourse of the 'hard' economy, and one which reinforces a narrative which places business growth as the key to long-term economic prosperity and resilience. In the remainder of this chapter, we will interrogate the assumptions which inform this narrative through reference to a range of quantitative and qualitative data sources pertaining to the CWCL. Quantitative data is aggregated from official statistics provided by, in the main, the Office for National Statistics and the Welsh Government Data Unit. With much of this data being published at the local authority level and without the possibility of disaggregation into parliamentary constituencies (and other such spatial units), it has been necessary to include indices for the whole of Powys in statistical measures of the CWCL. The qualitative data sources we draw on are the WISERD Localities stakeholder interviews carried out specifically in the CWCL and a series of interviews informing a study of local business practices and resilience in early 2009.

(De)constructing the mid Wales economy

Despite the territorial disparity between the CWCL and the central WSP area, they share a broad-brush socio-economic context which allows the CWCL to therefore provide a particular window for the study of (the) central Wales (Spatial Plan area). Moreover, our data collection within the CWCL, by unhappy coincidence, was undertaken at a time of unfolding worldwide recession. As such, predominantly quantitative data concerning the employment economy can be positioned and considered in dialogue with first-hand accounts detailing the initial effects, but, equally importantly, the variably anticipated impacts of the economic downturn. The dialogue between and within these data sources, therefore, may be read as a commentary on the multiple experiential constructions of the local economy. Further, we were provided with individual accounts which at once provided a commentary on 'official' narratives of the economy, and also offered insights into how the 'real economy' of mid Wales might fare and/or adapt in the face of change.

As such, and in keeping with our preceding discussion of the WSP, this section will be structured in accordance with the plan's three thematic priorities of communication, employment and labour market for the central Wales region.

Narratives of communication in the CWCL

It's obviously a sparsely populated area, with a very rugged landscape ... cut off quite a few times in the winter, and yet you've also got the coast line which is generally very mild. Rural, little or no heavy industry and, of high environmental quality … People, I would think, are probably more self reliant and they've had to be through generations … there's a recognition that they don't receive the same amount of public services as towns and cities do.

Given the physical terrain, low population density and a lack of industrial demand, as noted in the above quote, the transport infrastructure in much of mid Wales is comparatively underdeveloped, and, in some places, wholly lacking. For some respondents this situation had engendered a greater degree of claimed self-sufficiency and/or an expectation that transport services are, and inevitably will continue to be, comparatively lacking as a result of demographics, demand and topography.

The CWCL possesses a limited rail network beyond the main west–east arterial lines linking Aberystwyth, Newtown and Welshpool to the English Midlands, and the Pembrokeshire ports of Pembroke Dock and Fishguard to the M4 corridor in south Wales. This presents businesses in the locality with limited alternatives to commercial road haulage and heightens the requirement for a well-maintained highway infrastructure, a provision which was identified by many stakeholders as being lacking both in upkeep and new development:

Distribution and getting the product to market is very expensive for us. We don't have our own haulage department; in fact not many companies do these days. We farm it out to a third party who takes it up to the distribution hub in Oswestry. And from that hub, the product goes out to the retailers. In ideal world we would be there, down the central corridor to save costs. However, we are not and that is a disadvantage for us. The road link across central Wales is not the best, and I would hazard a guess that they are not going to build a motorway across it in my lifetime.

Specifically, the lack of dualled roads in the CWCL, coupled with a small threshold population and peripheral location from large urban markets, was repeatedly identified by stakeholders as among the overriding factors restricting business growth:

Biggest influence, accessibility, the argument that the A55 had to be dualled for service, open up the northern corridor … but you know, when you re-present that case on the southern corridor … the rules have been bent. The business case is not made, they say, but we all know there is an element of chicken and egg; if you haven't got communications, you won't get the investment.

These limitations in transport infrastructure, including local public transport services, create substantial obstacles for individuals living and working within the CWCL. Based on data returned in the 2001 Census, Ceredigion, Pembrokeshire and Powys all have a higher proportion of households owning a vehicle.[2] Taken individually, levels of access to these vehicles by household is highest in Powys (82.5 per cent), followed by Ceredigion (80.5 per cent) and Pembrokeshire (78.3 per cent) in turn. Compared to a national figure of 74 per cent, residents of the CWCL might collectively be considered as relatively transport-rich. However, several stakeholders noted how such figures should not be taken as a measure of deprivation (specifically, a lack of), but rather are indicative of limited public transport provision in rural mid Wales:

> I think the one thing I always harp on about is the rurality issue, the rural isolation and deprivation that's hidden within rural communities, and the way poverty is defined and measured doesn't actually pick this up ... One of the measures, you know, of poverty is if you've got a vehicle, but every single person out in these communities, even if it's a 40-year-old banger, they've got a car.

Indeed, only 2.7 per cent of the working population in the CWCL travel to their place of work by public transport, compared to an all-Wales figure of 6.5 per cent. However, this picture is at the same time complicated by lower than average numbers of people in the CWCL travelling to work by car or van either (63.3 per cent, compared to 70.2 per cent across Wales nationally). A number of factors might go towards accounting for this scenario, including a significant number of individuals walking or cycling to work, alongside others who actually reside at their place of employment. Here the latter group includes members of the agricultural community, as well as those engaged in forms of home-working across multiple sectors, with the greater daily flexibility afforded by home-based employment providing a way for working parents to better cope with limited child care services in rural areas.

One of the chief facilitators of home-working in recent times has undoubtedly been the internet. While recent figures for the UK as a whole suggest the extent of home-working has remained relatively constant since 2002, it is the case that the ongoing expansion and integration of ICT continues to create greater opportunities for participation in this practice. Groups highlighted elsewhere as being particularly likely to work at home include those in higher managerial posts and professional occupations and also the self-employed.[3] In regards to the latter, ICT has arguably increased the potential and opportunities for business start-ups, business growth and cottage industries, through, among other factors, reducing costs and widening access to a broader customer base:

> In terms of being in an out-of-the-way place, mail order has made this less of an issue, and even more so in the advent of the internet ... Having a worldwide presence through the website, you are reaching out to a far bigger audience than you were 20 years ago, when people would simply look in the Yellow Pages.

This was noted by several stakeholders as being particularly crucial for the CWCL's important tourism and hospitality sector, in terms of providing online

marketing and booking facilities. However, just as ICT has been accredited with
the capacity to encourage economic growth in localities, variability in its infrastructural provision has also been acknowledged as a spatial determinant of
development potential. Using data compiled by the Welsh Affairs Committee, the
highest concentration of registered broadband 'not spots' is shown to be in mid
Wales, with Ceredigion, Powys and Pembrokeshire collectively accounting for
47 per cent of all self-registrations in Wales as of August 2009 (Welsh Affairs
Committee, 2012: 46). Notwithstanding ongoing improvements in the telecom-
munications infrastructure across Wales (with the rate of 'not spot' registrations
dropping significantly in 2010 as compared to 2009) and a host of complementary
schemes to benefit online access in remote areas, mid Wales still suffers disproportionately poor ICT provision due to its peripherality. This inevitably limits the
potential for businesses (fledgling or otherwise) in the CWCL to fully exploit the
commercial opportunities which new technology can afford:

> This broadband issue ... the 'not spots' in the area ... if you're talking to
> businesses, that is one of the main things that they're finding extremely diffi-
> cult. People say that you can work anywhere these days, isn't it so ...
> However if you haven't got the broadband service, then that's a real big
> block for you. And farmers now, in particular, because of the way that the
> Single Farm Payment is being done, they have to do them online.

> Engaging with new technology I think is going to be key within this particu-
> lar sector, and indeed within so many economical sectors in Wales, where we
> get a boost from key markets which are difficult to reach, so we have to
> engage with digital media, social media, marketing, promotion, but in terms
> of business support, you know, one example shown up by the market
> research that we've done is, five years ago, 50 per cent of businesses in
> Wales had online facilities for people.

In addition to its potential business uses, 'the innovative application of digital
technologies' is promoted by the Welsh government as integral to 'delivering
affordable and sustainable services' in the context of current public sector spending cuts.[4] In particular, ICT is seen as a method of bolstering and widening service
delivery to remote areas and populations – providing access to everyday functions
including online banking, shopping and library resources, as well as supplement-
ing elements of health and social care provision through facilities such as NHS
Direct. On this basis, however, it is the case that a significant number of those
remote areas which stand to benefit most from such online resources are also
those areas which are currently subject to poor or non-existent broadband provision. Many residents in rural mid Wales, therefore, remain dependent on place-
based services and upon the varying forms of transport previously discussed.

The average travel times to a range of key services within all areas of the
CWCL (as aggregated from their constituent Lower Super Output Areas) are
significantly higher than the Welsh average in all instances. Notably, journeys to

libraries and secondary schools are particularly lengthy in comparison to national rates. With regards to individual authorities, it is apparent that Montgomeryshire suffers disproportionately, with travel times to transport nodes (train and bus stations) and primary schools being comparatively high.

Furthermore, the difficulties associated with limited access to services are often keenly felt by the elderly population, and here the CWCL is demographically over-represented in comparison to the Wales average. This is due in part, to the popularity of the Ceredigion and Pembrokeshire coastlines as retirement destinations for both Welsh and English in-migrants:

> If you look at Ceredigion ... you find that people move here when they retire. I think we have a disproportionate amount of retired incomers which have come probably from urban areas, and probably have an interesting and possibly sometimes unrealistic expectation as to what services might be available. They find it bizarre that there isn't a good public transport system you know or bizarre that they don't have a hospital that does heart transplants.

The proportion of older residents in mid Wales inevitably puts a comparative burden on service provision in terms of increased demand. This is compounded by comparative inaccessibility in many rural locations. However, this scenario also provides a boost to certain parts of the economy and the service industry. This is particularly so in the care sector, which has provided growth in employment opportunities in recent times and has become an increasingly important constituent of the labour market.

Narratives of employment in the CWCL

The WSP identifies the central WSP area as having comparatively low levels of unemployment. This observation is supported by data collected by the Office for National Statistics detailing the number of people claiming Job Seeker's Allowance (JSA) and National Insurance credits across the UK at monthly intervals. The claimant rate data for the three authorities within the CWCL, and Wales in its entirety, is conveyed in Figure 6.4, which illustrates the number of claimants in these areas as a percentage of the resident working-age population (ages 16–64 for males, 16–59 for females) for the period April 2005 to April 2011.[5]

While the claimant rate remained consistently lower in the CWCL than the average for Wales as a whole, Pembrokeshire was subject to the greatest level of fluctuation over the six-year period, with Powys following similar but less marked changes, and Ceredigion appearing a little more stable. This pattern was especially pronounced between April 2008 and April 2009 where, seemingly charting the onset of recession, the number of claimants per working resident population rocketed for all the local authorities under consideration, but particularly so in Pembrokeshire. Here, alongside the global economic downturn, the completion of major LNG construction projects around The Haven was cited as a significant contributing factor to Pembrokeshire's increased unemployment.[6]

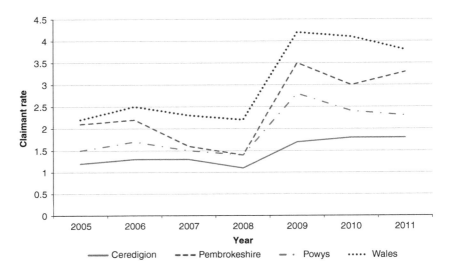

Figure 6.4 Claimant rate, 2005–11

Source: DWP Claimant Count, 2005–11.

Nonetheless, the claimant rate across the three CWCL authorities has remained significantly lower than the Welsh average since the onset of recession, with Ceredigion, in particular, maintaining the lowest rate across the whole of Wales at the close of 2009.[7] This apparent resilience of the mid Wales economy is supported by data compiled by the Wales Rural Observatory (WRO), which illustrates rural authorities in Wales (including the entire CWCL) as experiencing the lowest increase in claimant rates between July 2008 and July 2009, an increase of 1.3 per cent compared to increases of 2.6 per cent and 2.1 per cent in the valley and urban authorities respectively. A noted factor contributing to this scenario was that public sector employment – on which the WSP identifies mid Wales as being comparatively dependent – had thus far been relatively shielded from rising levels of unemployment prior to the Coalition Government's comprehensive spending review in October 2010.

Yet this assumption is problematic, insofar as it overlooks the significant spatial variation that exists between different rural areas as illustrated by Figure 6.4. Indeed, the most recent data on public and private sector employment by local authority[8] specifies Ceredigion as having the joint highest level of public sector employment in Wales (a figure of 35.6 per cent, equal to that of Anglesey). However, Powys and Pembrokeshire, by contrast, have figures ranking them among the lowest four Welsh authorities by this measure, at 25.1 per cent and 26.0 per cent respectively. At the same time, perceptions of public sector employment among stakeholders in the locality appear to vastly exceed these statistical measures: 'I read somewhere the other day that 80 per cent of the workforce in Ceredigion was public sector.' For many individuals living and working in mid Wales, the adjudged importance of the public sector resulted in very real concerns at the time of interview about the impact of the forthcoming government spending cuts, and the resilience of the economy as a whole:

> We're gonna need do more with less, there's no doubt about that. Looking at the economy, you don't need to be a John Harvey Jones to know that the public sector is going to be hit hard, and the private sector is going to find it difficult ... across the piste.

Following on, other characteristics of the mid Wales economy noted by the WSP in terms of business type and size may also contribute to its ability to cope, or not, with ongoing and predicted difficulties stemming from the recession context. For example, considering the types of both public and private enterprises operating within the CWCL, and using the Standard Industrial Classification (UKSIC) framework,[9] the proportion of agricultural local business units (LBUs) in each of Ceredigion, Pembrokeshire and Powys is higher than the all-Wales figure. This is most notable in Powys, where the percentage of agricultural LBUs is 37.1 per cent as compared to 33.2 per cent in Ceredigion, 24.9 per cent in Pembrokeshire and 13.6 per cent nationally. Despite the structural weaknesses in mid Wales's agricultural sector noted by the WSP, the aforementioned WRO report from October 2009 suggests that agriculture has fared better than other industries during the current economic downturn, with weakened Sterling having made products more competitive within the European market.

The next most significant enterprise base in the CWCL is property and business services, yet the proportion in all three authorities is between 5 and 7 per cent lower than the all-Wales average of 19.0 per cent, with this sector accounting for the highest number of LBUs at the national level. Also of note is the relatively low proportion of both retail and health sector businesses across the CWCL as compared to the national figures, while Pembrokeshire has a significantly higher proportion of hotel and catering businesses (10.9 per cent, compared to 7.7 per cent in Ceredigion, 6.3 per cent in Powys and 8.1 per cent nationally) due to its well-established tourism industry. As the WRO report also notes, rural businesses are facing significant challenges from the economic downturn across key sectors including retail, distribution and tourism, and this is particularly the case for small enterprises where tighter profit margins leave them vulnerable to cash-flow problems, indebtedness of mortgages and the risk of home repossessions. Statistically, the CWCL as a whole has a higher than average reliance on solo or small enterprises which employ four persons or less, coupled with a correspondingly low proportion of large enterprises employing 20 or more persons (see Table 6.1).

Yet, if opportunities for greater business expansion, as noted by the WSP, are restricted on the grounds of peripherality, accessibility and, thus, a limited customer base for goods and services, then the potential for retaining consistent

Table 6.1 Local business units according to size

	All VAT and/or PAYE-based local units	Persons employed			
		0–4	*5–9*	*10–19*	*20 or more*
Ceredigion	4580	75.5	13.1	7.1	4.3
Pembrokeshire	6365	71.2	15.9	7.5	5.5
Powys	9585	77.7	11.8	5.8	4.6
Wales	112,810	66.6	16.0	8.9	8.6

Source: ONS Inter-Departmental Business Register, 2010.

local trade is also greater for the same reasons. From this perspective, geographical marginality was repeatedly invoked by mid Wales business owners as affording a degree of insulation from wider national and international economic trends, and providing a degree of job security on these grounds:

> In the boom times we don't get the extreme highs that the cities generate. On the plus side, come the downturn, like we are experiencing now, the market is generally more stable. We don't get the highs and lows so much; it stays on a much more even keel.
> We're not too interested in too much expansion. It's so much easier to stay as you are, make a tidy living; because you can make a tidy living here. If you've got one shop and it's making money and you don't want to risk it, why do it? You don't have to expand.

As noted in the latter quote, the idea of business expansion as necessarily desirable is challenged not only in terms of being an unnecessary risk in the current context, but also as surplus to the lifestyle requirements of some people who choose to live and work in the CWCL; a sentiment echoed by other stakeholders we interviewed:

> There are four of us who work full time here, and all four of us own our own tiny little homes. We would want to develop business so that everybody could remain secure and not have to worry about whatever mortgage they might have. But we are not in the business in order to get a Bentley in five years' time. We have good employment in a business we love, and as long as the business continues with a little bit of growth to cover inflation, rises in living costs and utility bills, we won't complain.

These trends in business size and type are also seemingly reflected in working patterns, with a high average rate of self-employment across the three CWCL authorities of 22.0 per cent as compared to the all-Wales average of 12.2 per cent in 2010.[10] This preponderance of self- and, to a lesser extent, part-time employment[11] may, on the one hand, reflect the lack of population mass in the locality required to attract large employers:

> We do not have any major house builders in the area. The majority of our customers are jobbing builders. Small businesses: either guys working on their own or small companies with a few employees. A lot of the property around here is old and constantly needs repair or renovation, and that is our core business. We do not get the volume of new builds as you do in urban areas, and we rely on small works, especially given the way the housing market is at the moment, where people are looking to renovate rather than relocate.

At the same time, higher levels of self- and part-time employment provide a loose characterisation of aspects of the labour market and residents' needs and (lack of) choices, with it noted, for instance, that people living in parts of the CWCL often need to undertake multiple jobs due to low pay and/or limited availability of full-time work. These factors will be further considered in the following section.

Narratives of the labour market

Turning to the condition of the labour market in mid Wales, figures accrued by the Annual Population Survey indicate that Montgomeryshire, Ceredigion and Pembrokeshire all have a higher than average proportion of skilled tradespersons at work, including those in agricultural, electrical, construction, food preparation trades and artisan crafts (see Table 6.2). Locally, there are significant variations within the CWCL, with technical occupations significantly higher in Pembrokeshire (and specifically south west Pembrokeshire) than across Wales as a whole as a result of the well-established petro-chemical industry developed around Milford Haven. Montgomeryshire has a comparatively high proportion of residents working as managers and senior officials, which may well reflect proximity to the west Midlands and multiple labour market opportunities. Finally, Ceredigion has the highest percentage of people working in professional occupations across the CWCL and also marginally higher than the national average, indicating the presence of the relatively large higher education sector in the county.

 Further breaking this down in terms of skill levels across the labour market, the Annual Population Survey data determine the proportion of residents of working age with formal (NVQ level) qualifications in Ceredigion, Pembrokeshire and Montgomeryshire, and for Wales as a whole. Ceredigion was home to the highest proportion of working-age residents with qualifications at NVQ levels 1, 2, 3 and 4; with the most significant difference over the other CWCL areas being at level 3+ (A/AS level and above) as a reflection, in part, of the presence of Aberystwyth and Lampeter universities. Montgomeryshire, however, underperforms in comparison to Pembrokeshire and the all-Wales figures — which are roughly comparable — in terms of formal educational accomplishment, possessing instead the greatest proportion of working-age residents with other types of

Table 6.2 Percentage of people by occupational classification

	Montgomeryshire	Ceredigion	Pembrokeshire	Wales
Managers and senior officials	19.3	12.1	11.7	13.2
Professional occupations	10.8	13.8	8.0	12.8
Associate professional and technical occupations	10.8	13.4	12.4	14.6
Administrative and secretarial occupations	8.0	11.7	8.3	10.5
Skilled trades occupations	15.2	15.0	16.7	11.7
Personal service occupations	9.6	7.9	12.4	10.3
Sales and customer service occupations	8.4	7.3	8.0	7.5
Process, plant and machine operatives	8.9	3.8	8.1	7.6
Elementary occupations	8.7	15.1	13.8	11.2

Source: Annual Population Survey, 2010.

qualification. Similarly, Montgomeryshire had a higher than average rate of people with no formal qualifications, at 14.6 per cent compared to 14.1 per cent across Wales nationally, while Pembrokeshire was marginally below average at 14.0 per cent and Ceredigion significantly lower with only 10.2 per cent of working age without formal qualifications.[12]

Despite levels of educational and vocational attainment being demonstrably and statistically variable across the CWCL, a common shortcoming of mid Wales, as identified in both policy discourse and our various interviews, is the inability of businesses to secure skilled labour to meet specific demands:

> As far as production and administrative jobs, we don't have a problem ... With a little bit of on-site training they can cope with the task at hand. But there is a serious need for good-quality engineering staff. You just cannot get them in this area. But certainly, when we looked for engineering staff nine months ago we found we had to look far afield. In terms of technical staff ... and by this I mean those who test the quality of our product, they are very difficult to come by. As a small business, we are now looking at 'growing our own' and taking on an engineering apprentice, but it is a big commitment.

The above comment, made by a representative of a manufacturing concern and significant local employer, highlights the problems faced by businesses in parts of mid Wales as regards to hiring staff with specialised – but by no means niche – skill sets. In this instance, the firm in question has resorted to apprenticeships and 'growing their own' skilled employees, which evidently places a considerable burden on company resources. Many other (often smaller) firms, however, do not have the capacity to follow this example, and here a restricted local labour market can undermine both sustainability and the potential for growth.

If investment in training provision is a costly, but necessary, proviso for businesses in mid Wales and beyond, a relatively underdeveloped HE/FE sector, outside of a number of larger settlements in the CWCL, presents a mountable challenge to regional competitiveness. Limited levels of accessibility to centres of training and education provision mean that the capacity of many residents, and members of the workforce, in mid Wales (and beyond) to attend these institutions is relatively limited. With mid Wales generally characterised by low population density and small settlement size, it lacks the critical mass to support additional 'physical' centres for HE/FE training provision. For this reason, e- and/or satellite learning takes on an increased importance in the CWCL vis-à-vis other localities in Wales and particularly so following the economic downturn, with a lack of available jobs encouraging many young people to remain in education:

> More young people have returned to the sixth form and FE college than ever before. So people are avoiding entering the labour market by erm, quite rightly, you know, seeking to improve their qualifications and go back into and remain in education.

Yet the attainment of higher qualifications and skills is in itself no guarantee of finding employment in the locality. It is certainly the case that, statistically, the CWCL has a lower proportion of the working population in the 25–49 age bracket as compared to the national average, and that both Pembrokeshire and Montgomeryshire hold a similarly below-average fraction of 16–24 year olds (whereas Ceredigion hosts a large resident student population). At the same time, the over 65s are over-represented across the CWCL as compared to the Wales average (see, for example, the Annual Population Survey).

While the ageing demographic profile does not directly talk to the educational attainments of the resident population of the CWCL, or to the levels of skills and training held by the workforce, it does reflect the opinions and perceptions of many stakeholders, a large number of whom cited an inability to retain young achievers (whether native or resident learners in HE/FE institutions) on the basis of limited career opportunities:

> Obviously you've got, you know, the most educated get their A levels, do well. I mean they tend to, to move away, you know, Cardiff probably … Holding on to them I think is a long-term problem which is an economic regeneration issue.

Expanding on this point, the loss of bright and ambitious young adults is widely seen as an historical, predominantly rural problem which cannot easily be rectified through policy intervention.

> I hear people often saying, 'Well, the countryside's problem is its depopulation, people leaving the countryside, moving to go to live in London or Cardiff, that's tragic,' like it's something that's only just started happening. It's been happening for a century and a half. I do believe it's a response to the lack of chances that are to be had in these towns so people who have education, and skills, ability, ambition, they tend to move away.

This passage reiterates a common understanding that mid Wales functions as a popular retirement destination and not as an economy capable – or indeed suited – to attracting and accommodating the vocational and lifestyle preferences of young professionals. However, there is also a common alternative discourse which holds that individuals and families reside in mid Wales on the grounds that they are prepared to accept perceived shortcomings in services, access and opportunities for upward mobility as the pay-off for an enhanced quality of life.

> There are people who stay there and do some kind of trade-off between the income they get with what people call lifestyle factors. But I don't feel that this is purposeful coping. It is not choosing to do this, but the absence of a choice to do anything else. So they survive, and they continue to live.

For a number of stakeholders, including the above, there exists an understanding that the social and environmental benefits of living in mid Wales may go some way in mitigating restrictions relating to limited facilities and career pathways. This perspective, however, comes out of an understanding that remaining in mid Wales is not so much a lifestyle choice, but rather the outcome of restricted opportunities and material circumstances. In contrast, a number of other stakeholders were more positive in their assessment of mid Wales as a vibrant place to live and work, suggesting that many people actively choose to remain in, or relocate to, the CWCL. This, it was argued, demonstrated the capacity for environmental and quality-of-life factors to outweigh the apparent constraints of living and working in a peripheral economy.

Conclusion

Peripherality (in both national and wider UK contexts), rurality and concurrent issues of limited internal and external communications infrastructures were repeatedly invoked by differently placed stakeholders as the key issues shaping multiple, sometimes competing, narratives of the mid Wales economy. These issues, drawn into focus by the recession context, are well documented in official policy discourse including and beyond the WSP (e.g. *One Wales: Connecting the Nation*, Welsh Assembly Government, 2008b; *National Transport Plan*, Welsh

Assembly Government, 2009; *Delivering a Digital Wales*, Welsh Assembly Government, 2010a), where they are as acknowledged as placing limitations on business growth potential, in terms of expanding current enterprises, attracting new (larger) enterprises and investment, and accessing wider markets for goods and services. However, it was also recognised by stakeholders within the CWCL that substantial improvements to the regional transport network, in particular, were unlikely to take place in the short- to and mid-term. It was anticipated by many respondents at the time of interview that this scenario would be further compounded by public sector spending cuts and therefore no obvious policy interventions would be able to pragmatically address these structural shortcomings, placing the onus on the business community to cope, develop and adapt accordingly.

Furthermore, with the mid Wales economy dominated by small-scale enterprises, often lacking the scope but also desire for expansion (as emphasised by several stakeholders), the capacity to provide opportunities for younger residents with varying levels of skills and qualifications is seemingly highly limited. Similar restrictions apply in terms of the ability for industry in mid Wales to attract highly skilled in-migrants and, with them, possibilities for knowledge transfer and innovation at the grass roots level. On this basis, the job market in mid Wales can be considered as relatively stagnant and, indeed, there is an apparent disjuncture between the skills required by some of the businesses we spoke to and the skills possessed by young adults who are moving elsewhere (whether by choice or necessity) in search of employment opportunities. At the same time, HE provision in mid Wales remains geographically uneven, being concentrated in specific micro-localities, with institutions serving a limited range of knowledge and skills which may not align fully with the needs of local industry.

Current national policy (e.g. *Skills That Work for Wales*, Welsh Assembly Government, 2008c) challenges higher education providers in Wales to become much more deeply engaged in supporting future economic success through stronger relationships with business and the commercialisation of new and existing knowledge. There is arguably a need for this to go further still in mid Wales, in terms of developing a greater alignment of educational provider activity with sector priorities which would require enhanced capacities for employer engagement in curriculum design. Yet these are longer-term initiatives, requiring a perspective and commitment beyond the immediate financial pressures and constraints being imposed on stakeholders, and their customers and constituents alike, by the recession:

> Our relationship with those multinationals has essentially been as a host community to their processing. We are trying to change that relationship and we see Pembrokeshire Technium as a gateway for them to access not only Welsh higher education but UK higher education ... our vision is very much that of utilising the Technium and the structures, the land, the science park and the effect it created around it as a centre of applied technology trying to connect the needs of industry, marine and energy in particular, with the

research capacity and capabilities of Wales and further afield. So that is our vision and that is the way that we feel we can grow the knowledge, economy, incubate and spin out businesses. We fully understand that this is not a five-year or ten-year programme; it is a 20- to 30-year programme.

The above points tally with the aims and objectives of a dominant discourse, reproduced through the WSP, on the needs of the mid Wales economy to expand its workforce and to capitalise on innovation and efficiency gains engendered by up-skilling. Sustainable development potential is also allied with the need to enhance internal and external ICT and transport infrastructural networks (see also *Economic Renewal: A New Direction*, Welsh Assembly Government, 2010b) However, this is conceivably a double-edged sword insofar as greater access to outside markets may bring increased competition and vulnerability to fluctuating economic cycles which have been held at bay, to an extent, by mid Wales's peripherality.

It is important, therefore, that the positive aspects of a localised economy in terms of the stability of an established customer base, knowledge of and respon-siveness to customer needs, flexible working patterns (i.e. through self-employ-ment) and the availability of more environmentally sensitive (low-carbon) products and services – cumulating in a potentially greater resilience to the multiple challenges of recession, climate change and peak oil (*A Low Carbon Revolution*, Welsh Assembly Government, 2010c) – are not overshadowed by an overarching and spatially undifferentiated emphasis on economic growth above all else. This has been demonstrated through locality-situated narratives, which variously prioritise factors including growth, expansion, opportunity, security risk, resilience, culture and lifestyle, and which, in dialogue with official statisti-cal measures, combine to present a more nuanced yet ultimately partial snapshot of the contemporary mid Wales economy. A complex space, it is one which often challenges common-place assumptions regarding the political economy in (and of) rurality, and also one which sets a distinct context for the ways in which reces-sion unfolds through people's lives and livelihoods.

Notes

1 This quote is derived from the CWCL stakeholder interview programme. All subsequent quotes in this chapter are also taken from these interviews.
2 Percentage of households without a car or van, 2001 InfoBaseCymru/ONS.
3 National Centre for Social Research Omnibus Survey, 2008.
4 Source: Welsh Assembly Government (2010), Delivering a Digital Wales: The Welsh Assembly Government's Outline Framework for Action. http://gov.wales/docs/det publications/101208digitalwalesen.pdf. Accessed: 20 January 2011.
5 These figures are derived from mid-year population estimates which are compatible with the 2001 Census, and while claimant count data is available for LSOAs, recorded rates at this level have a greatly increased margin for error and have not been included on this basis.
6 Source: http://www.westerntelegraph.co.uk/news/4085409.Pembrokeshire_unemployment_ on_the_increase/. Accessed 19 May 2015.

7 A figure of 2.1 per cent in December 2009. Source: Local Government Data Unit, Wales.
8 Compiled by Wales Assembly Government, year ending 30 June 2010.
9 Includes all PAYE and VAT-registered businesses.
10 Wales Assembly Government figures for year ending 30 June 2010.
11 The same data set gives the part-time employment rate, where Powys matches the Wales average of 25.9 per cent and Ceredigion and Pembrokeshire are slightly higher, at 29.3 per cent and 27.2 per cent respectively.
12 InfoBase Cymru/ONS.

References

Davies, C. (2006) *The Welsh Language: The Story of Britain's Oldest Living Language*. Ceredigion: Y Lolfa Cyf.

Day, G. and Hedger, M. (1990) 'Mid Wales: missing the point', *Urban Studies*, 27(2), 283–90.

Day, G., Rees, G. and Murdoch, J. (1989) 'Social change, rural localities and the state: the restructuring of rural Wales', *Journal of Rural Studies*, 5(3), 227–44.

Halfacree, K. (2006) 'Rural space: constructing a three-fold architecture', in Cloke, P., Marsden, T. and Mooney, P. (eds), *Handbook of Rural Studies*. London: Sage.

Haughton, G., Allmendinger, P., Counsell, D. and Vigar, G. (2010) *The New Spatial Planning*. London: Routledge.

Hoggart, K. (1990) 'Let's do away with the rural', *Journal of Rural Studies*, 6, 245–57.

Jones-Evans, D., Thompson, P. and Kwong, C. (2011) 'Entrepreneurship amongst minority language speakers: the case of Wales', *Regional Studies*, 45, 219–38.

Madgwick, P., Griffiths, N. and Walker, V. (1973) *The Politics of Rural Wales: A Study of Cardiganshire*. London: Hutchinson.

Marsden, T. (1998) 'New rural territories: regulating the differentiated rural spaces', *Journal of Rural Studies*, 14, 107–19.

Marsden, T., Murdoch, J., Lowe, P., Munton, R. and Flynn, A. (1993) *Constructing the Countryside*. London: UCL Press.

Scott, A., Christie, M. and Midmore, P. (2004) 'Impact of the 2001 foot-and-mouth disease outbreak in Britain: implications for rural studies', *Journal of Rural Studies*, 20, 1–14.

Welsh Affairs Committee (2012) *Broadband Services in Wales*. London: TSO.

Welsh Assembly Government (2004) *People, Places, Futures: The Wales Spatial Plan*. Cardiff: Welsh Assembly Government.

Welsh Assembly Government (2008a) *People, Places, Futures: The Wales Spatial Plan Update*. Cardiff: Welsh Assembly Government.

Welsh Assembly Government (2008b) *One Wales: Connecting the Nation. The Wales Transport Strategy*. Cardiff: Welsh Assembly Government.

Welsh Assembly Government (2008c) *Skills That Work for Wales: A Skills and Employment Strategy and Action Plan*. Cardiff: Welsh Assembly Government.

Welsh Assembly Government (2009) *National Transport Plan*. Cardiff: Welsh Assembly Government.

Welsh Assembly Government (2010a) *Delivering a Digital Wales: The Welsh Assembly Government's Outline Framework for Action*. Cardiff: Welsh Assembly Government.

Welsh Assembly Government (2010b) *Economic Renewal: A New Direction*. Cardiff: Welsh Assembly Government.

Welsh Assembly Government (2010c) *A Low Carbon Revolution: Wales' Energy Policy Statement*. Cardiff: Welsh Assembly Government.

Welsh Rural Observatory (2009) *The Impacts of the Current Recession in Rural Wales*. Available at: http://www.walesruralobservatory.org.uk/sites/default/files/THE%20IMPACTS%20 OF%20THE%20RECESSION%20IN%20RURAL%20WALES%20-%20FINAL% 20Oct%2009.pdf. Accessed: 15 March 2013.

Western Telegraph (2009) Significant increase in Pembrokeshire unemployment, 29 January. Available at: www.westerntelegraph.co.uk/news/4085409.Pembrokeshire_ unemployment_on_the_increase/. Accessed: 15 March 2013.

Woods, M. (2011) *Rural*. Abingdon: Routledge.

7 New localities in action and reaction

Martin Jones, Scott Orford, Jesse Heley and Victoria Macfarlane

Wales: a heterogeneous and divided nation?

This book has been about the WISERD locality research programme, which has operated in the context of a devolved Wales. The spatial backdrop has initially been the Wales Spatial Plan (WSP) and its fuzzy boundaries, and more recently notions of 'spatial complexity' associated with the Williams *Commission on Public Governance and Delivery*. As detailed in Chapter 2, the WSP provided a temporary spatial fix for developing a devolved Wales and a means of instructing regions how to behave economically and culturally in terms of mobility, movement and connection. The 'new localities' approach to spatial development has challenged simplistic understandings of regions based on drawing lines on maps and suggesting that governance complexity can be simplified by merely introducing coterminosity; instead our approach has focused attention on processes of 'locality-making', or the ways in which semi-stabilised and popularly recognised representations of locality are brought into being through the moulding, manipulation and sedimentation of space within ongoing social, economic and political struggles.

Analysis of secondary data from official sources in Chapter 3 has revealed a nation that can be divided geographically along demographic, socio-economic and cultural lines with clearly demarcated sub-regions that are persistent across different data domains and various thematic analyses. The mapping of these data at various commonly used statistical spatial units helps not only to convey these divisions, but also to create and maintain a narrative that informs a conventional reading of Wales that was discussed in Chapters 2 and 3. It was this reading that helped inform our choices of localities and the themes that were the focus for the in-depth research. But it is also apparent that this conventional statistical reading of Wales is at odds with the *heterogeneity and complexity of the localities* that emerged from the stakeholder interviews in Chapters 4, 5 and 6. Although many of the variables show strong spatial patterns, such as deprivation indices in the Heads of the Valleys, this was not always reflected on the ground and stakeholders often criticised the negative and oversimplified characterisation that can emerge from statistical representations of Wales. This may, in part, be an artefact of the types of variables traditionally used to map Wales. An analysis of the

'Living in Wales' attitudinal data constructed an alternative picture, for instance, one that broadly mapped onto other classifications created by metrics such as deprivation indicators but which told a slightly different story (Orford and Jones, 2010). Nevertheless, this does not mean that there is no truth in what the statistics are saying, simply that there are other ways that Wales can be represented and framed outside of 'official' representations.

This tension between the official and statistical and the tacit and personal was unpacked in the three localities chapters. In Chapters 4, 5 and 6, the authors provide an in-depth analysis of three localities in Wales: those of the Heads of the Valleys, the A55 corridor and Central and West Coast (CWCL) respectively. Identified on the basis that they could (and perhaps would) provide a counterpoint to an historical narrative of Wales-as-a-region (see Chapter 2), these case studies also put paid to the notion of Wales having any clear-cut regional compositions (which are certainly not fixed). Undoubtedly, the political project of transforming Wales's regional identity within the United Kingdom into that of a nation *with* regions has gone some way in dispensing a regional framework of governance (Heley and Jones, 2012); nevertheless the extent to which this has been (or will continue to be) institutionalised is open to question. Here the WSP represents a clear thread between the three empirical chapters, serving as a means of characterising the different spatial contexts of Wales as they have been envisioned by the Welsh government, and as a blueprint on which to transpose our own findings. It is not, however, the purpose of this book to point out where 'official' depictions of Welsh regions and localities in an era of devolution are either incorrect or incompatible with the experiences of those living and working in Wales. Our thinking seeks to contribute to understanding the *heterogeneity and complexity of localities* and we return to this now by revisiting some of the conceptual propositions from Chapter 1.

The 'new localities' debate and doing geography

Locality can be seen, first, as bounded territorial space, which is recognised politically and administratively for the discharge and conduct of public services, and for the collection and analysis of statistical data. Second, locality represents a way of undertaking comparative research analysis, linked to processes occurring within the locality and also processes shaping the locality from the outside and, most importantly, connecting localities. This allows for the historical analysis of a given locality over time. Third, locality can be used to read spaces of flows for numerous policy fields, which in turn exhibit spatial variations due to interaction effects. The object of analysis here is the policy field and not the locality *per se*. This reading of locality is sensitive to localities being defined by their cores rather than by the total area, such that the boundaries might be flexible and fuzzy (Jones and Woods, 2013).

Building on this, for the concept of locality to still have analytical value, we would suggest that it must be possible to attribute observed processes and outcomes to social, economic and political formations that are uniquely configured in a given locality, and this, we argue, requires a locality to possess both material and imagined coherence. We are drawing inspiration here from, but not deploying, cultural political economy (CPE) (see Jessop and Sum, 2001). CPE emphasises the interplay of economic and cultural 'imaginaries' (i.e. narrative elements that provide senses of coherence and identity). The 'imaginary' is not to be understood as opposed to or distinct from reality; it structures a landscape in which individual goals are situated and political projects can be pursued. By material coherence, then, we refer to the social, economic and political structures and practices that are uniquely configured around a place. Thus, material coherence may be provided by the territorial remit of a local authority, by the geographical scope of an economic development initiative, by the catchment area of a school or hospital, by a travel-to-work area, by the reach of a supermarket or shopping centre, or by any combination of the above and other similar structures and practices. Material coherence hence alludes to the institutional structures that hold a locality together and provide vehicles for collective action.

By imagined coherence we mean that residents of the locality have a sense of identity with the place and with each other, such that they constitute a perceived community with shared patterns of behaviour and shared geographical reference points. Imagined coherence, therefore, makes a locality meaningful as a space of collective action. There are territorial units that exhibit material coherence but lack a strong imagined coherence – notably artificially amalgamated local authority areas – and there are territories with an imagined coherence but only a weak material coherence, either through fragmentation between local authority areas or integration into larger socio-economic administrative structures. We would not consider areas falling into either of these categories to be strongly functioning localities.

Both material coherence and imagined coherence are also important in fixing (through multiple intersections) the scale at which localities can be identified. The imagined coherence of a locality is framed around perceived shared behaviours (such as using the same schools, hospitals, railway stations, supermarkets; being served by the same local authority; supporting the same football or rugby team; or attending the same 'local' events or joining the same 'local' branches of organisations) and shared geographical/historical reference points (recognition of landscape features; knowledge of local 'characters'; memories of events in 'local' history), but it is 'imagined' in that it is not founded on direct interpersonal connection (see Anderson, 1991). In this it differs from the social coherence of a neighbourhood – which may share some of the above attributes but is framed around the probability of direct interaction between members – and from the imagined coherence of a region – which is a looser affiliation that draws more on perceived cultural and political identities and economic interests.

Similarly, the material coherence of a locality should be denser and more complex than that found at a neighbourhood or regional scale, since the material coherence of a neighbourhood will be restricted by its situation within a larger geographical area for employment, administrative and many service provision functions, and the material coherence of a region will be fragmented by the inclusion of several different labour markets, local authority areas, sub-regional shopping centres, etc.

Through the process of data auditing and stakeholder interviews, it has become clear that particular spatial constructs and material conditions actively serve to set apart Welsh localities, while others serve to bound them together and undermine feelings of difference. In regard to both the A55 corridor and the CWCL, common narratives are those of an outstanding national landscape and a strong rural heritage. Corresponding with the profile of mid and north as provided in the WSP, which identifies these factors as key in driving forward high-value tourism, stakeholders tended to juxtapose these more idyllic descriptions with the problems wrought by limited access and isolation.

Bringing attention to these more problematic aspects of daily life in many parts of rural mid and north Wales, local authority workers in particular had a tendency to highlight the problems of providing education and health care. In regard to the latter, this was often articulated in terms of supplying health care to a growing number of elderly residents, many of whom had, apparently, chosen to retire to the Welsh countryside. Indeed, in-migration driven by environmental and quality-of-life factors was also identified as a key factor in shaping locality in both the A55 corridor and the CWCL, although it was seemingly more contentious in the former. Here the growing intensity of cross-border relations on the north east border with England was occasionally cited as undermining the coherence of a 'Welsh cultural heartland', this being strongly allied with the use of the Welsh language.

For many stakeholders in the north and mid Wales localities, however, the key issues shaping their outlooks were those related to the economy. Both sets of stakeholders gave emphasis to the ongoing importance of agriculture and primary industry, and a substantial number expressed the opinion that this dominance would remain, given the limited potential of rural areas to attract large-scale inward investment by larger-scale manufacturing concerns. On a related point, many respondents cited a relative lack of employment prospects in many parts of rural mid and north Wales as the principal force behind the comparatively high levels of out-migration among younger age groups (see Heley et al., 2012). However, limited job options represented only one (albeit predominant) factor in this process, and a number of stakeholders also highlighted a related tendency for younger people to leave rural Wales for the purpose of attending university. The 'pull' of the urban in terms of culture and lifestyle was also raised by some stakeholders as a long-standing factor to consider in terms of the imaginative and material processes at work in shaping Welsh localities

If economic conditions and employability emerged as important themes in our discussions of place and locality in the A55 corridor and the CWCL, then they took centre stage in the Heads of the Valleys case study. Undoubtedly – and given the timing of the interview process – the impacts of recession and the so-called 'credit crunch' loomed large in the collective consciousness of the interviewees, but the majority of respondents provided a much more long-term view based on their own professional knowledge and personal experiences. For those in the

Heads of the Valleys, their responses were often in contrast to media, public and policy perceptions of the area as blighted by educational underachievement, skills shortages and economic inactivity. Certainly, these concerns were raised by interviewees in each of the three case study sites, and by stakeholders working across the full spectrum of policy areas. However, and as is made clear in Chapter 4, the negative and excessively oversimplified characterisation of the valleys as a space of worklessness and limited opportunity overlooks significant social and economic heterogeneity. Likewise, a portrait of north and mid Wales centred on landscape, rurality and identity provides only a partial account of the experiences and shifting understandings of those inhabiting these spaces, and on this basis it is hoped that this account goes a small way in addressing this critical gap in knowledge.

Interviewees also described narratives of engagement in their everyday work that reached out beyond this delimited space to multiple external sites. For example, interviewees in Ceredigion talked not only about places within the county, but also about neighbouring areas of Pembrokeshire and Gwynedd, the administrative centres of adjacent local authorities, and the Welsh capital, Cardiff. These, to quote Savage (2009: 3, emphasis added), are 'granular spaces' where,

> People do not usually see places in terms of their nested or relational qualities: town against country: region against nation, etc. *but compare different places with each other without a strong sense of any hierarchical ordering.* I further argue that the culturally privileged groups are highly 'vested' in place, able to articulate intense feelings of belonging to specific fixed locations, in ways where abstract and specific renderings of place co-mingle. Less powerful groups, by contrast, have a different cultural geography, which hives off fantasy spaces from mundane spaces.

The notion of multiple external sites is also powerful in north east Wales and can be read along the A55 in relation to developments such as the Mersey Dee Alliance (MDA). Formed in April 2007 – now comprising the local authorities of Cheshire west and Chester, Denbighshire, Flintshire, Wirral, Wrexham, and the Welsh government, and Merseytravel – MDA recognises that the area represents a single economic sub-region with a population of close to 1 million and is imagined to be unique in the UK as a major economic area divided by a national boundary. The area has a great diversity of businesses and a metro economy as well as a large rural hinterland and coastal commuter belt and is a major contributor to the UK economy. According to interviewees, partners agree to work together on common strategic interests to ensure a sustainable future for the area, and facilitate a coherent approach to social, economic and environmental issues. The MDA, therefore, addresses the strategic, cross-boundary issues that affect the area as a whole so as not to duplicate local activity and to ensure it creates added value. Its cross-border national geography (Wales–England), though, provides an obstacle to becoming a city-region (see below).

The uneven geographies of the south east Capital Network region represent a challenge for dissecting the interrelationships between material coherence and imagined coherence, and for locality management on a practical day-to-day basis. As noted in Chapter 4, this region is three distinct spaces – the Heads of the Valleys Plus, Connections Corridor and the City Coastal Zone. The first is distinctly absolute and bounded for residents with accessibility concerns, unable to travel to, and for, work. The second is differently relative and based on making connections. The third is a textbook space of flows, where transport networks and traditions of social and economic interdependence allow for increased interconnectivity and movement. The close proximity between the latter two sub-regions (Corridor and Zone) has been a driving force behind a city-regions debate in Wales, which, from 2014, has effectively replaced the WSP as the 'territorial fix' for doing economic development in post-crisis Wales (Etherington and Jones, 2009). This initiative shift is, of course, not peculiar to Wales, and is being used across the globe as the way to pin down the local in the post-crisis global (see Galland, 2012).

Mindful of the need to play to the relational geographies of south (east) Wales and promote growth-oriented policy instruments, the Welsh Government Minister, Edwinda Hart, established a 'task and finish' group in November 2011 to consider the potential role of city-regions in the future economic development of Wales. The task was to decide, on the basis of objective evidence, whether a spatially focused city-region approach to economic development, as opposed to the (national) WSP, could deliver an increase in jobs and prosperity for Wales. Drawing on evidence mainly from Europe and north America, where strong regional economies have developed over the past 30 years and are perceived to be associated with a close relationship between economic agglomeration and strong city-regional structures of governance (compare Cheshire et al., 2014; Cooke and Morgan, 1998; Fujita and Thisse, 2013; Glaeser, 2008; Storper, 2013), the three reasons for adopting a city-region approach are noted as: improving the planning system; improving connectivity; and driving investment through a stronger and more visible offering from an agglomerated wider region (see Welsh Government 2011:11). A final report, published in July 2012, argued that:

> *City region boundaries must reflect economic reality and not political or administrative boundaries. Genuine engagement and meaningful collaboration across many local authorities will be needed.* This will certainly involve ceding power, funding and decision making to a more regional level.
> (Welsh Government, 2012: 7, emphasis added)

Clear, here, are considerations for the fixing of material coherence and imagined coherence, which is not considered a 'short-term fix' (ibid.: 11), but one recognising that 'different levels of governance are required for different policies' (ibid.: 10). Two distinctive city-regions were proposed – south east Wales (Cardiff, described initially for 'external promotion purposes' to distinguish Cardiff from neighbouring Newport, and later renamed the 'Cardiff Capital Region' to acknowledge both capital city status and the stretched-out variegated geography of city-region building) and Swansea Bay Region – with support given to strengthening the MDA, with the proviso being that all this has to be about creating urban engines and power-houses of growth by harnessing the beneficiaries of transport, housing, inward investment and funding opportunities. In the words of a private sector representative from the Cardiff business community:

> The argument against is purely parochial. It is well proven that the ability to operate at scale and in a co-ordinated manner delivers higher economic output. My view is that city regions are essential if we really want Wales to maximise its potential. Manchester is a smaller city than Bristol but has seamlessly linked with adjoining towns to create a Greater Manchester city region. In terms of international profile and ability to capitalise on this, Manchester is able to deliver in a way that Bristol probably doesn't. This point is amplified when one considers the case of Cardiff and Swansea. Cardiff as a city region needs to get to that scale, as well as Swansea for west Wales.
>
> (Kevin Beevers, Director of Commercial Lending,
> Julian Hodge Bank, quoted in Barry, 2014: 15)

At the time of writing, there is much debate over two areas of city-region building. First, the 'south Wales Metro' – a transport initiative proposed as a means of connecting two sub-regions (City Coastal Zone and Connections Corridor) to the Heads of the Valleys Plus (see Barry, 2012) and whether governance and delivery can be effective, given the networked complexities of this policy intervention and its impacts on planning, housing and the spatial structure of urban development in south east Wales. Second, whether the Enterprise Zones (EZs) (Central Cardiff and St Athan–Cardiff Airport being two of seven, alongside Anglesey, Deeside, Ebbw Vale, Snowdonia and the Haven Waterway in Pembrokeshire), revealed in 2011 and launched in 2012, alongside 21 EZs in England, can be effective in providing a 'new localist' (Clarke and Cochrane, 2013) agglomeration fix for the city-regions. The argument here, similar to the debates on EZs in the 1980s and 1990s, is not just one of transparency (how the sites are performing – see National Assembly for Wales, 2013), but also one of deadweight and displacement – poor value for money and high costs of job creation due to no-new-activity *per se* but the spatial and territorial relocation or diversification of economic activity to take advantage of financial incentives and tax breaks. For instance, during the 1980s, around £300 million was spent on 11 zones where some 4,300 firms employed 63,000 workers, but the new jobs created amounted to just 13,000, which works out at £23,000 a job, perhaps £50,000 in today's money (Hildreth and Bailey, 2012: 28). It is not clear how far new EZs in Wales will avoid such previous failures.

A key question for locality-making is how this city-regions agenda, based on capturing the shape of the knowledge-based economy, plays out along the implementation of the recommendation from the Williams Commission pertaining to spatial complexity and the territorial reshaping of the 22 local authorities. At the time of writing (June 2015), public services minister Leighton Andrews is leading the post-Williams drawing of a new map for local government, which is promising fundamental reform, but struggling with questions of economies of scale (territorial size and overall number) and economies of scope (local preferences for voluntary mergers and delivery of quality). There is an inevitable tension here between the preferences of constituencies, the scale of efficient provisions of public goods and regulation, and the relational making of attributes of Wales's cities into jurisdictions. Storper (2014) has captured these tensions in research on leading regions in north America, and the implications apply equally to Wales, as these tensions help to explain why social and economic governance seems to move forward in a haphazard way, through a process of 'tinkering whilst the economy burns' (Heley and Jones, 2012). And, on the economy, this book has not discussed in any detail the historical (see Lovering, 1978) or current industrial structure of Wales, in terms of how this relates to employment distributions, or Wales's economic position relative to the rest of the UK, but, in the context of Wales's future devolution and whether the economy will ever be robust enough to allow a greater degree of independence from neighbouring England and its porous borders, the commentary by Jenkins still holds and needs to be tackled:

> [T]he Welsh economy since devolution has moved to bottom of the UK's 12 regions. Growth moved in step with that of the UK as a whole between 1970 and 1990, but since then it has slumped: real income in the UK has grown by 42% and in Wales by only 27%. One in five Welsh households is now below the poverty line and among children the figure is an extraordinary one in three. These are dire statistics. This has further increased Welsh dependency on government in general. Roughly 60% of Welsh domestic product is public spending, against roughly 50 in Scotland and 40 in England. A quarter of Wales's workforce is employed by the state. The £9bn in UK-wide welfare paid to Welsh families means that benefits have risen in the past 25 years from a quarter to a third of household income.
>
> (Jenkins, 2014: 28)

Future research: moving the 'new localities' debate forward

Currently, we have analysed the stakeholder interviews for the two tiers in each locality. What we have not yet done is a cross-locality analysis of interviewees in the same tier and policy area. Such a cross-locality analysis could reveal important insights into how different national (Welsh and Westminster government) policies play out across space and place, depending upon local context. It was evident from the baseline audits, statistical mapping and the stakeholder interviews that demographic, socio-economic and cultural pressures affect the three localities differently, and a cross-locality analysis would allow us to unpack the intersection between population needs and policy demands. Here, the WSP, and the now-live city-regions, as frameworks for policy implementation, could provide an important analytical tool for understanding and interpreting cross-locality differences, in the same way as it has helped frame the interpretation of the stakeholder interviews within each locality.

The current analysis has also started to generate new questions relating to the interplay between people, policy and place within the context of the 'new' localities debate, as has the ever changing political, economic and social landscape in

Wales. In order to chart how stakeholders, and their related policy areas, are coping with the continuing economic downturn, the cuts to budgets and essential services and the continued transfer of powers from Whitehall to Cardiff, it is necessary to return to some of the stakeholders for follow-up interviews. These interviews will form an important continuity and allow longitudinal analysis of the impact of devolution on Wales at different scales and policy arenas.

The analysis has also started to emphasise the importance of stakeholders beyond Tiers 1 and 2. A detailed mapping of stakeholders who constitute Tier 3 (civil society such as the voluntary sector; NGOs; churches; trades unions), Tier 4 (private sector representatives) and Tier 5 (grass roots organisations, local social movements) in each locality followed by interviews with an indicative sample would provide further empirical and analytical insight into how policy and locality map vertically as well horizontally between localities. This deep rich vertical mapping is currently missing from the locality analysis, although the stakeholders we have interviewed have helped highlight some of the issues that affect Tier 3, 4 and 5 stakeholders with respect to their policy areas.

The WISERD Civil Society funded centre presents an ideal opportunity to undertake this research, building on the first phase of WISERD programmes of work. There is certainly a need to undertake a comparative study of stakeholder and civil society organisational involvement in Wales's two city-regions, Swansea Bay Region and Cardiff Capital Region, noted above. This involves several interrelated research questions. How do these changes affect and involve civil society organisations? What are the narratives of devolution and community engagement in the city-regions? How are these being worked into policies and procedures for stakeholder engagement? Who is involved in this 'new localism' and does this relate to forms of associational life and political engagement? What are the compositions of the city-region boards, and their sub-groups and other structures of engagement? How successful is the city-region project in realising its objectives of economic and social empowerment?

The study has also used several innovative mapping techniques to represent the spatial patterns in the data. These techniques have gone beyond conventional cartographic rendering of thematic maps to include cartogrammatic renderings of population spaces and qualitative mapping using spatial ellipses to render places discussed in stakeholder interviews. These various mappings have allowed unorthodox visual representations of Wales through both statistical and non-statistical lenses and have challenged the well-defined territories constituted by the WSP and commonly used spatial units of analysis, such as unitary authorities. Indeed, the ellipses provide a novel and unique representation of policy spaces in each locality, ones that often cross unitary authority boundaries despite many policy arenas being a function of a single administration. What is needed now is a more detailed and rigorous comparison of the elliptical spaces and policy areas within and between localities. Mapping the spatial ellipses onto existing administrative areas would provide a deeper understanding of how well-defined formal territories, such as unitary authorities, interact with and impact upon, policy-makers and practitioners in their daily tasks. It will also provide further empirical grounding in the way the material and imagined coherence of the localities play out spatially with respect to the underlying governance and administrative structures. This will be especially interesting in the context of city-region-building in Wales, the recommendations of the Williams Commission (if these are implemented) and any changes to territorial governance as a result of the Wales Bill in 2015 and 2016.

A development of the qualitative GIS would be the construction of spatial metrics to enable a quantitative spatial analysis of the interview transcripts to complement and support the qualitative analysis. Simple straight-line and network distance measures between the workplace of the stakeholder and the places mapped in their interview will allow descriptive statistical analysis to be undertaken and comparisons to be made of the spatial relationships between stakeholders, policy areas and localities. Some of these relationships have already emerged from the qualitative analysis of the interviews and have been treated discursively in chapters 4, 5 and 6. A statistical treatment of these relationships will support these findings as well as further a deep empirical understanding of the material and imagined coherence of the localities by different stakeholders. For instance, it may be possible to analyse the concept of 'local' and how this can vary by policy and geographic context by linking the coding of the concept in the qualitative analysis with spatial metrics generate by the GIS. This will allow the concept to be mapped both in terms of its meanings and also its spatial extent within and beyond the locality.

A recurring theme in this study has been the importance of pre-existing administrative and statistical units of analysis in framing both the localities debate and the selection and analysis of the three locality case study areas. Although we have already discussed the problems and limitations of using these units for defining and analysing the localities in the context of bounded and unbounded, fixed and fluid, defined and fuzzy spaces, and have demonstrated in chapters 4, 5 and 6 that stakeholders' work often means that they go beyond the boundaries demarcated by official geographies, they are still important for understanding the social-spatial structure of Wales and how the localities fit into this configuration. This is because official statistics continue to be invariably published for standard statistical and administrative geographies and this constrains the types of geographies that can be used in the statistical analysis of localities. Chapter 3 demonstrated this well, although it also showed that non-standard cartographies can be used to render different visual representations of Wales. Locality studies would benefit immensely from the ability to assemble bespoke statistical geographies that more precisely map onto stakeholders' and others' spatial conceptualisation of locality, especially if this affords a move towards more unbounded and fluid geographies. However, the experience of operationalising the fuzzy boundaries in the WSP by using aggregations of Lower Super Output Areas demonstrates the problems of reconciling geometric and non-geometric territories.

Nevertheless, there may be ways of addressing this issue with the increasing use of micro-level data in social science research. Here, the data is not published for pre-designated spatial units but rather is available at the individual level.

Typically, this raises issues of disclosure, meaning that the data is not freely accessible but rather can be accessed via a safe setting, such as the Economic and Social Research Council's Secure Data Service (SDS), the Office of National Statistics' (ONS) Virtual Microdata Laboratory (VML), or the Administrative Data Research Centre Wales (ADRC-W), that allows researchers access to administrative data records. Although there remain substantive issues relating to geographic disclosure in the use of these records, they do pave the way to the opportunity to create bespoke units for statistical analysis that better map onto non-statistical definitions of locality. In addition, the programmes of data linkage that are associated with micro-data services will increase the number of longitudinal datasets, which will enable analysis of how localities change through time. Moreover, a move away from cross-sectional data analysis of standard spatial units to longitudinal analysis of bespoke regions may also provide a basis for the statistical analysis of fuzzy and fluid spaces, something which is difficult with current data provision.

References

Anderson, B. (1991) *Imagined Communities: Reflections on the Origin and Spread of Nationalism*. London: Verso.

Barry, M. (2012) *A Cardiff City Region Metro: Transform/Regenerate/Connect*. Cardiff: Institute of Welsh Affairs.

Barry, S. (2014) 'City region can be a game-changer for Wales', *Western Mail*, 24 April, 15.

Cheshire, P. C., Nathan, M. and Overman, H. G. (2014) *Urban Economics and Urban Policy*. Cheltenham: Elgar.

Clarke, A. and Cochrane, A. (2013) 'Geographies and politics of localism: the localism of the United Kingdom's coalition government', *Political Geography*, 34, 10–23.

Cooke, P. and Morgan, K. (1998) *The Associational Economy: Firms, Regions, and Innovation*. Oxford: Oxford University Press.

Etherington, D. and Jones, M. (2009) 'City-regions: new geographies of uneven development and inequality', *Regional Studies*, 43, 247–65.

Fujita, M. and Thisse, J.-F. (2013) *Economics of Agglomeration: Cities, Industrial Location and Globalization*. Cambridge: Cambridge University Press.

Galland, D. (2012) 'Is regional planning dead or just coping? The transformation of a state sociospatial project into growth-oriented strategies', *Environment and Planning C: Government and Policy*, 30, 536–52.

Glaeser, E. L. (2008) *Cities, Agglomeration and Spatial Equilibrium*. Oxford: Oxford University Press.

Heley, J. and Jones, M. (2012) 'Regionalism in Wales', in Ward, M. and Hardy, S. (eds), *Changing Gear: Is Localism the New Regionalism?* London: Smith Institute.

Heley, J., Gardner, G. and Watkin, S. (2012) 'Brave new localities? Cultures of local economy in a Celtic fringe region', *European Urban and Regional Studies*, 19, 366–82.

Hildreth, P. and Bailey, D. (2012) 'What are the economics in the move towards LEPs?', in Ward, M. and Hardy, S. (eds), *Changing Gear: Is Localism the New Regionalism?* London: Smith Institute.

Jenkins, S. (2014) 'A chance for Wales: can the slumbering dragon awake?' *Guardian*, Journal, 30 September, 27–9.

Jessop, B. and Sum, N. L. (2001) 'Pre-disciplinary and post-disciplinary perspectives', *New Political Economy*, 6, 89–101.

Jones, M. and Woods, M. (2013) 'New localities', *Regional Studies*, 47, 29–42.

Lovering, J. (1978) The theory of the 'internal colony' and the political economy of Wales' Review of Radical Political Economics 10, 55–67.

National Assembly for Wales (2013) *The Record of Proceedings, 30/04/2013*. Cardiff: NAW.

Orford, S. and Jones, S. (2010) 'Mapping Welsh neighbourhood types classified using attitudinal data from the national Living in Wales survey', *Journal of Maps*, 346–53.

Paasi, A. (1996) *Territories, Boundaries and Consciousness*. Chichester: Wiley.

Savage, M. (2009) *Townscapes and Landscapes*. Mimeograph. York: Department of Sociology, University of York.

Storper, M. (2013) *Keys to the City: How Economics, Institutions, Social Interaction, and Politics Shape Development*. Princeton, NJ: Princeton University Press.

Storper, M. (2014) 'Governing the large metropolis', *Territory, Politics, Governance*, 2, 115–34.

Welsh Government (2011) *City Regions Task and Finish Group: 'City Regions' Definition and Criteria*. Cardiff: Welsh Government.

Welsh Government (2012) *City Regions: Final Report*. Cardiff: Welsh Government.

Index

A55 corridor 96 (fig); bridging function 95, 97; connectivity 97; cost 97; locality 95–115; and micro-localities 97, 98
accessibility *see* mobility and accessibility
age band distribution 45, 51, 46–50 (figs)
agriculture, Central and West Coast Locality 133

Better Wales.com strategic document 33
birthplace: outside Wales 99–100, 100 (fig); in Wales distribution 51, 52 (fig)
border flows 110
boundaries, Williams Commission 6
business relocation and global factors 88, 91
business sizes: by unitary authority 60–1, 61 (table); Central and West Coast Locality 133–4, 134 (table)

Capital Network region 148
cartogram: description 43; interpretation 45
central Wales: characteristics 127; Wales Spatial Plan 123, 126–7
Central and West Coast Locality 118–40, 119 (fig); agriculture 133; business sizes 133–4, 134 (table); communications 127–31; commuting 129; demographics 131, 137; economy 121–2; employers 122; employment 131–5; home-working 129; industries 121–2; internet broadband provision 130; labour market 135–8; occupation types 135, 136 (table); policy spaces 123, 125–6, 124–5 (figs); politics 121; population 121; public sector employment 132–3; qualifications 135–6; self-employment 134–5; training provision 137; transport 128; travelling times 130–1; unemployment rates 131–2, 132 (fig);

vehicle ownership 128–9; Wales Spatial Plan 122–3; Welsh language 120–1
central-local relations 26–30; delivery of public services 28–30; Labour Party binds 28; 'policy development deficit' 28; public services review (Simpson) 30; six-regions proposal 30, 31 (fig); Welsh polity size 27–8
city-regions: advantages 148; and Enterprise Zones 149; proposed 148–9; report (2012) 148; and Williams Commission 149–50
civil society organisations 151
claimant count rates, by unitary authority 63, 63 (table)
coherences 145
College, The, Merthyr Tydfil 88–9
communications, Central and West Coast Locality 127–31
community regeneration 112–14; 'churn effect' 112
commuting: by unitary authority 64–5, 64 (fig); Central and West Coast Locality 129; local 100; North Wales to England 98–9, 99 (table)
cross-boundary sub-region 147
cultural political economy 145

data: mapping 143–4; micro-level 152–3; tensions between 144
demographics 43–54; age-band distribution 45, 51, 46–50 (figs); birthplace in Wales distribution 51, 52 (fig); Central and West Coast Locality 131, 137; lone-parent households distribution 54, 55 (fig); long-term limiting illness distribution 51, 54, 53 (fig); population distribution 43, 45, 44 (fig)

For Product Safety Concerns and Information please contact our EU
representative GPSR@taylorandfrancis.com
Taylor & Francis Verlag GmbH, Kaufingerstraße 24, 80331 München, Germany